APOCALYPSE
ON THE SET

APOCALYPSE ON THE SET

Nine Disastrous Film Productions

BEN TAYLOR

Overlook Duckworth
New York • London

This edition first published in hardcover the United States and the U.K.
in 2012 by Overlook Duckworth, Peter Mayer Publishers, Inc.

NEW YORK
141 Wooster Street
New York, NY 10012
www.overlookpress.com
For bulk and special sales, please contact sales@overlookny.com

LONDON
90-93 Cowcross Street
London EC1M 6BF
inquiries@duckworth-publishers.co.uk
www.ducknet.co.uk

Copyright © 2012 by Ben Taylor

PHOTO CREDITS:
*All images appearing in the text are courtesy of Photofest NYC
unless otherwise indicated.*

Cataloging-in-Publication Data is available from the Library of Congress.

A catalogue record for this book is available from the British Library.

Book design and typeformatting by Bernard Schleifer
Printed in the United States

10 9 8 7 6 5 4 3 2 1

ISBN 978-1-59020-188-6 (US)
ISBN 978-0-7156-4327-3 (UK)

for Holly

Contents

APOCALYPSE
ON THE SET

Introduction

THERE IS NOTHING EASY ABOUT MAKING A FILM.

When a production begins to unravel, the brutal rules of a zero-sum game take hold. The ultimate accomplishment of completing the picture reflects the reverse image of a relentless struggle. The memories of endured hardships are as lasting as the narrative itself and become linked to a film's director, cast, crew and studio.

Each of the films discussed in this book is distinguished by its disastrous production. These films were also chosen for the diverse circumstances of their production troubles, which provide insight into the incalculable combination of problems and dangers that take such a toll on the people involved in the process of filmmaking.

Many of the dark events that unfurled throughout the making of these films bear an uncanny resemblance to the equally bizarre stories woven into their scripts, accentuating the irregularities and uncertainties of real life in comparison to the balanced plots of fiction. I have endeavored to explore the making of these films and their interior narratives whenever this may provide a deeper understanding of the craft of filmmaking. However, the information in each chapter adheres to published interviews, memoirs, magazine articles, newspaper articles, production footage, documentaries and other published materials.

This book is not meant to serve as a protracted tabloid exposé. It is my intention to contribute to an understanding of the rigorous nature of creating a story on celluloid and the business of making movies. This is a business that combines art, money, ego and power into productions that are ephemeral and original in nature, thus presenting a unique set of problems. It is these uncommon problems of filmmaking that are found at the intersection of art and money, where the inspiration of ideas and themes must shoulder enormous financial burdens while striving to *entertain*—from the Latin *tenere*, to literally "hold" the audience.

Though all of these films put many people under incredible duress, they were all ultimately completed. Audience response was highly influenced by the sometimes heavily publicized strife of the filming process. The stories of the characters within the film were often secondary to the rumors of disaster and misfortune that enticed many to see these pictures. When applicable, this allure will be discussed more fully. A complete history of some of these films warrants an examination of the forces acting outside the nucleus of the film's production, specifically how problems unrelated to the film itself can interrupt progress. Often forces within the media, studio politics or tumultuous bad luck shadowed a project from beginning to end.

Additionally, the allure of many of these productions is not just due to the events that transpired during the making of the film. In many cases, the crisis behind the movie was one of conflicting personalities or a crisis of ego. Despite the multitude of problems that can arise on a set, many of the most troublesome were the personal dynamics between cast, crew and studio. Very often incredible tensions existed between one man's vision and the interests of the people who carried the burden of realizing that vision.

Each chapter will explore the variety of strange and unforeseen circumstances that affected the making of these films. The nature of the struggle changes from one film to another, but there is a common fortitude among those who labored so tenaciously to see their projects through to the end.

Introduction

The following nine chapters recount the plight of those caught within the storm of a deteriorating production. In the chapter on *Pulgasari*, a Korean filmmaker is held prisoner and forced to realize the brash visions of his dictatorial captor, Kim Jong Il. The making of *The Abyss* poses the unique problem of completing an entire film under water. The endless production of *Apocalypse Now* drags a determined director into the darkness and strain of a jungle odyssey. A budget spiraling out of control and holding a studio hostage is the disaster that earned *Heaven's Gate* its notoriety. Production is halted after the accidental death of the lead actor in *The Crow*. Filming abruptly shuts down on the set of *Twilight Zone: The Movie* after a disastrous helicopter crash. The brutality of the lead actor in *Fitzcarraldo* leads a destitute director to threaten death. An unending array of catastrophes build from the first day of production on *The Adventures of Baron Munchausen*, a movie shadowed by special effects problems and studio fury. Interminable expenses and forces of nature cripple a 166-day shoot on the set of *Waterworld*.

When strung together, these chapters provide a kaleidoscopic exploration of the unique nature of the movie business. The eras, genres and people that make up each film highlight the common urge that embattled filmmakers increasingly feel to surrender to the fatalistic circumstances of a film held captive by misfortune or outside influences. What remains inspiring is that each of these movies reached completion under the tremendous inertia of despair. Though the motivation to finish the films came in large part from financial obligations, the persistence and bravery of those involved cannot be ignored.

Just as viewers of the final cut are invited to be captivated by the struggle of the protagonist, those who follow the misadventures of these cinematic endeavors will discover that truth is stranger than fiction, reality more volatile than narratives, and fate more improbable than plots.

1

The Last Shot of the Night

Twilight Zone: The Movie

Brink of Eternity

ILMMAKING is a pursuit often undertaken in a search for supremacy. Each movie must be greater than the last; it must be louder, more explosive and more daring than any other. If this bravado could be manifest in a physical form, it would undoubtedly look a lot like a man named Joe Bonomo, one of Hollywood's earliest stuntmen. His father immigrated to the United States from Istanbul, Turkey, and Joe was born in Coney Island. Joe would later joke that when his father arrived in America he must have mistaken the torch of the Statue of Liberty for an ice cream cone, thus inspiring him to start Bonomo's Ice Cream. While forging his business, his father fell in love with a French woman who operated a family candy store with her father. They eventually married, believing their life together to be as natural a union as the joining of their confectionary businesses.

Bonomo's scrawny build as a child gave no indication of his parents' sugary livelihood. Mercilessly teased for his thin frame, Joe aspired to become a perfect physical specimen from an early age.

This aspiration was not at all uncommon in the family. His great uncle Yousiff, known to many as "The Terrible Turk," was once a champion wrestler and had earned a respectable fortune. Yousiff never trusted banks, so he kept his winnings with him in the form of gold pieces secured within a pocketed belt that he wore at all times. However, Yousiff's refusal to ever part with his winnings eventually brought about his demise. He was traveling aboard the S.S. *La Bourgoyne* when a fierce storm hit. The ship began to sink, and he leapt into the water, allowing others to take safety in the few lifeboats available. With his considerable strength, he certainly could have swum to safety, but only if he had released the hefty pouch from his waist. For Yousiff, the gold was far too dear to part with. He sank into the icy waters of the Atlantic with his shining coins still anchored to his waist. In his memoir, Joe reflected, "I think I learned a great lesson from that . . . the accumulation of money has always been a secondary consideration."[1]

After being shuffled from one high school to another, and earning varsity letters in football, basketball, track, wrestling, swimming and hockey, Joe finally decided to drop out. He continued his bodybuilding, and he soon became the prototypical image of virility. He appeared in one photo series wearing nothing but a leopard-skin loincloth, single-handedly hoisting a barbell into the air. In time, he discovered that his physical prowess could lead to a rewarding career, just like it had for his great uncle Yousiff. But he wasn't interested in being a career prize fighter. Instead, he became entranced with the glamorous life of stuntmen. His cavalier attitude and kinesthetic intelligence led to numerous jobs leaping from buildings and jumping from speeding trains on Hollywood sets. These brave feats contributed to the mystique of his personality. As Bonomo himself put it, he was a man who "teetered on the slippery Brink of Eternity." In the opening chapter of his memoir, he warns, "The story of my life is going to make such a crazy, mixed up,

impossible sounding affair that you either won't believe it and catalogue me as a congenital liar—or you *will* believe it and recom-
mend me for psychiatric treatment." While the story of his life does
not seem quite as "impossible" as he makes it out to be, it certainly
is unusual.

Bonomo's greatest asset was his judgment. He was never one to
shy away from a challenge, yet he always remained committed to the
exhaustive calculations and professionalism required to complete a
dangerous stunt safely. One day, he was called upon by a director to
leap from a rope ladder dangling from an airplane onto the top of a
speeding train. The stunt was not unusual for him, but he recalled,
"I just didn't like the looks of the guy who was to pilot for this stunt."[2]
Joe declined to do the jump. The agitated director jabbed, "What's
the matter with you Bonomo, running out of gas?" Instead, another
stuntman, who was a close friend of Bonomo's, came in to do the
scene, but Joe warned him, "Don't go up. I've got a bum hunch about
this pilot." He said, "I'll never forget that look in his eyes. It seemed
to tell me that he knew I was right."[3] The stuntman ignored his own
misgivings and agreed to do the job.

First, the inexperienced pilot flew next to the train instead of
above it, as he was directed to. The stuntman was slammed against
the side of the carriage several times as he tried to climb the flimsy
ladder to safety. He may well have survived those injuries had the
pilot not made another attempt at the stunt, oblivious to the hyster-
ical shouts of the cast and crew on the ground. Without any radio
communication to the pilot, they could only watch in horror. The
second pass was too much for the battered stuntman to endure. After
being dragged against the metal siding of the train at seventy miles
an hour, he let go and fell to the ground with "almost every bone in
his body sticking out through his flesh in jagged splinters."[4] As the
cast and crew rushed toward him, he uttered his last words to the
director, "I'm sorry I missed, Bill." The pilot, still circling in the air,

undoubtedly saw what he had done. Joe looked up to the sky and watched as "the plane just flew away."

The day of the accident stayed with Bonomo all of his life, through a career that left him with numerous film credits and thirty-seven broken bones. The stuntman's death was an early indicator of the insatiable appetite shown by Hollywood directors as they increasingly urged actors to inch a little closer to the "brink of eternity." Though Bonomo wrote of the incident in 1968, it was virtually ignored by anyone outside the production. The public and many members of the filmmaking industry remained ignorant of the dangerous, sometimes negligent, attitude of directors in relation to their stuntmen until 1982, when the horrific events surrounding *Twilight Zone: The Movie* became national headlines.

Indian Dunes

In the early morning hours of July 23, 1982, producer and director John Landis was preparing to shoot the final scene of a short film that would be one of four vignettes that collectively made up the feature film *Twilight Zone: The Movie*. It was a complex action scene designed to look like a wartime aerial attack on a Vietnamese village. The shoot was in Indian Dunes Park, located thirty-five miles north of Los Angeles. A Bell UH-1B helicopter N87701, registered to Rocky Mountain Helicopter, Provo, Utah, had been painted dark green to give the chopper the authentic look of a U.S. Huey warship.

The lead actor, Vic Morrow, was to portray a soldier making a final gesture of bravery by carrying two young Vietnamese orphans across a shallow body of water as the village behind them was obliterated by the explosive firepower of the helicopter above. It was the last day of shooting and the final scene in the film. Numerous delays had pushed the production over schedule; everyone was tired and anxious for a wrap. Among those most desperate to complete the scene were Renee Chen and Myca Dinh Le, the two children playing the young orphans. Only a little darkness remained; in a few hours the sun would rise, the shooting would be complete, and they could all go home. Earlier in the night, Morrow tried to ease Chen and Le's anxiety about their upcoming scene by making silly faces. They both giggled.

A cluster of eleven bamboo huts, representing the village, was rigged to explode by the special effects technician. In response to a crew member's concern about the dangerous size of previous explosions filmed during the shoot, Landis responded, "You think that was big? You ain't seen nothing yet!"[5] The camera operator warned Landis about debris from the final explosions hitting the helicopter. Landis quickly dismissed the remark by responding sarcastically, "We may lose the helicopter."[6]

Six cameras were placed around the action, and Landis, armed with a megaphone, gave the directive to begin the scene. The helicopter began to hover over Morrow as he made his way across the water with a child in each arm. Landis shouted for the helicopter to fly lower and then gave the order for the technician to explode the mortars hidden within the village huts. As the fireball explosion rose into the air, the tail rotor of the helicopter was engulfed in flames and the pilot began to lose control. The helicopter's searchlight swung in all directions as the pilot wrestled with the craft. It began to spin wildly, descending toward the water where Morrow and the two children struggled to reach the safety of the shore. As the explosion of the village continued behind it, the helicopter's fuselage crashed into the water, crushing Renee. Then the spinning blades struck Morrow and Le, decapitating both of them.

In an instant, three lives were lost. One of the most horrific accidents in the history of film had just occurred, and the mock village continued to burn. Filming was shut down. Ambulances and police arrived at the scene. The parents of the children were distraught and screaming. The pilots emerged with only a few minor injuries, mostly cuts and bruises.

As the days passed, many of those involved slowly realized the scope of the disaster and the significance of those lost lives. The lingering question was simple, though the answer was elusive: Where exactly did things begin to go wrong? As the sun began to rise over Indian Dunes, the lamentable outcome of the previous night became a clear and terrifying reality, which would echo through years of protracted litigation.

An American in Yugoslavia

Like so many other directors, Landis's filmmaking career was built upon a tremendous amount of resourcefulness in working the Hollywood system, and a little bit of luck. He was born in Chicago in 1950 and raised in the Westwood section of Los Angeles. While living in this epicenter of the film industry, he became intrigued with motion pictures. Perhaps while sitting in the darkness of the movies, he realized that writing and directing was to be his station in life. He was a restless, volatile young man, and his education included stints at several different public schools. "I'd get A's and F's," Landis recalled.[7] The chain of unsuccessful academic ventures concluded with John's brief tenure at the Oakwood School, a private institution in North Hollywood. John's lasting mark was renaming the school newspaper the *Oakwood Gorilla*. Decades later, the paper still retains Landis's title, now simply referred to as the *Gorilla*. For John there was no sense in waiting to embark on the career he was determined to have. Landis first landed a job in the mailroom of 20th Century Fox, and determined to make it to the top through sheer force of will.

Landis took steps to ensure that if the opportunities did not come to him, he would go to them. He did exactly that when he learned that a Clint Eastwood war movie, *Kelly's Heroes*, was going to begin production in Yugoslavia. Landis reassured family and friends that he had been offered a job on set, when in actuality no one attached to the production knew who he was. He assumed that appearing on the set would earn him a menial job, so he made his way to Yugoslavia. The producers were duly impressed with Landis's resolve and hired him as an assistant. Landis recalled, "My time on *Kelly's Heroes* was full of adventure." One day a friend brought him to meet his old friend Salvador Dali. "Dali drew a sketch of me in felt-tip on a pink linen napkin! I asked if I could have it. He said yes, for $800—impossible on $60 a week and no expenses. So he kept it, and I was devastated. On the drive back to Umag, Gabby told me not to be silly and always to 'separate the art from the artist.' This advice I've put to good use since."[8]

After the filming concluded, Landis traveled to Europe, where he worked for two years on the sets of various spaghetti westerns. Though these genre films formed the foundation of his professional career, Landis's ultimate inspiration came from the whimsical, indulgent monster movies that he loved as an adolescent. An early infatuation with the macabre was the basis for his unique style of horror: a meandering approach that never seems to take itself seriously. Landis returned to the United States in 1971 and attempted to turn his script *Schlock* into a feature film. A modest budget of $60,000 was an appropriate sum for a film that was crafted to take self-effacing jabs at the ridiculous, low-budget monster movies of Landis's youth. A distributor picked up the final product, but the film never earned the profits or recognition Landis had hoped for. Instead, people seemed more interested in the notion of someone as young as Landis—he was twenty-one at the time—directing a feature theatrical release. It was this novelty that landed him an invitation as a guest on *The Tonight Show* with Johnny Carson. Yet, despite this brief period of notoriety, Landis would quickly fall back into the shadows.

After years of pitching film ideas to studios while scratching and clawing his way to greater opportunities, Landis was finally contacted by Jim Abrahams and David Zucker, who had written a script they called *Kentucky Fried Movie*, a loosely strung collection of simple comedic skits aimed to satirize television and popular culture. Landis watched their ten-minute demo reel and agreed to direct the picture. After being turned down by several studios, they eventually raised $1 million from various independent sources. The film came out as a summer release in 1977, and it managed to garner a modest profit and equally modest praise. A *Time* magazine review remarked that the film expresses "the hope that television is not bending to the breaking point all the young minds exposed to it. . . . There is a lot of good sense of humor in its assaults on television and the movies' sillier realms."[9] In a flash of premonition, the reviewer unknowingly predicts Landis's next movie when he wrote that the film "is a sort of National Lampoon's that talks and moves." Shortly after *Kentucky Fried Movie*, Universal placed a $2.7 million bet on a film of little expectations called *Animal House*, Landis's third directorial effort. The film grossed $200 million. Landis was just twenty-eight years old. Perhaps this early success had the effect of halting his development. His unflinching, raw look at the sloth of college life was richly rewarded. His youthful demeanor was now his most important asset for directing films geared toward a newly identified demographic.

His appetite free to grow unchecked by the studios, eager to claim his next picture as theirs, Landis became a victim of his own success. One producer remarked, "He's so arrogant. He's his own worst enemy. But he has a reason to be arrogant. He's the most talented director I've worked with. You love John or you hate him."[10] The studios had their minds made up. They loved him and were ready to satisfy his every whim. His next feature, *The Blues Brothers*, was the story of two brothers on "a mission from God" to reunite their band. It was a simple framework from which to hang numerous chase scenes, explosions and dance routines. No expense was too great. The production required 300 car crashes involving 120 stunt cars, 60 of which were destroyed. One of the most apt descriptions comes from critic Roger Ebert, who observed, *"The Blues Brothers* is the Sherman tank of musicals."[11] Ebert goes on to say that the film "cost untold millions of dollars and kept threatening to grow completely out of control."

The sound and spectacle of *The Blues Brothers* suggest that a large part of Landis's style is born out of the bravado of youth. Each scene strives to outperform the last, as if the director is imploring the viewers to gaze in awe at the orchestra of destruction he has the power to conduct. The result was a film that would bring in over $57 million in domestic receipts. It seemed as long as the numbers kept adding up, Universal was willing to turn a blind eye to the rumors of recklessness surrounding Landis's special effects and stunt sequences.

His next project was a relic from his past, titled *An American Werewolf in London*. Having written it years earlier, Landis was finally in a position to direct his own material. Once again, Universal agreed to distribute the film, but Landis, perhaps anxious to escape the watchful eyes of studio suits, collected $10 million from several independent sources to finance the project. Though the film earned less than his earlier feats, it did rise to profitable territory, while retaining Landis's accomplished sense for action, mayhem and gore beneath a thin veil of dark humor. It was his unique, brazen approach to storytelling that earned Landis praise from audiences and industry moguls alike. One notable admirer was Steven Spielberg, who was anxious to embark on a joint effort with Landis.

Another Dimension

When Warner Bros. mentioned an ambitious project to adapt Rod Serling's 1960s-era television show *The Twilight Zone*, Spielberg leapt at the opportunity. It was finally a chance for the two of them to collaborate on a picture, a goal they shared since first meeting after the success of *Animal House*. The press had already made note of Landis's induction into a growing fraternity of young directors who were commanding salaries and privileges once reserved for the elite veterans of Hollywood. In a review of *An American Werewolf in London*, *Newsweek* writer Jack Kroll identified Landis as "a member of the wise-guy generation of movie directors. . . . What they see through that camera is not so much the real world as other movies, which they parody, put on, take off and otherwise play with like the brilliant kids they are."[12] Landis's contract for *Twilight Zone: The Movie* reflected his meteoric rise to success. For this film, he would stand shoulder to shoulder with Spielberg, acting as coproducer. His salary, a relatively modest sum of $150,000, was a pleasant after-thought compared to the potential income he was poised to receive with the five gross profit points he was awarded. Landis was also granted the coveted right of final cut, allowing him to make virtually all artistic decisions on his portion of the film under the condition that it remained within the boundaries of a PG rating.

The near limitless control bestowed on Landis was common among proponents of the auteur theory of filmmaking. French film critic and theorist André Bazin first explored the idea of the director as the "author" of the film. This theory, popularized first in the 1950s, suggests that the director is the sole commanding visionary behind the work and the lone architect of the mise-en-scène. The French term *mise-en-scène*, literally translated as "putting on stage," can mean everything that is placed within the camera lens, including the actors, set and props. Though the term has many interpretations and definitions, the mise-en-scène could be thought of in this sense as the completed canvas of the director's efforts. French film critic Alexandre Astruc elaborated the analogy through the idea of the director's *caméra-stylo*, or the "camera-pen." This theory suggests that the director is more of a storyteller than a screenwriter, dominating the screen with his or her singular creative strokes.

However, some do not buy into this theory. As writer and director David Mamet explained, "On the set, the male director is traditionally addressed as 'sir.' This can be an expression of respect. It can also be a linguistic nicety—a film worker once explained to me he'd been taught early on that 'sir' means 'asshole.' And, indeed, the opportunities for tolerated execrable behavior on the set abound."[13] He also said, "Whom is the film 'by'? Spend a day on the set and you learn. It is by everyone who worked on it." In regard to Landis's imperial command over the shoot, it is difficult to know who held the greater belief in the auteur theory, Landis or the studio. It seems both were content with the hierarchy that held the director king above cast, crew and perhaps reason. So long as the box office numbers ascended to majestic heights, Landis was ruler.

One person all too thrilled to be inducted into Landis's court was veteran actor Vic Morrow, slated to be the lead in Landis's segment. Born in 1929, the Bronx native had early aspirations to become an actor. Morrow looked for acting work while supporting himself as a taxi driver, eventually showing up to an open casting call for an MGM movie called *The Blackboard Jungle*. Morrow caught the attention of the producer and director, outdoing numerous others who auditioned, including a young Steve McQueen. His impressive debut won him a long-term contract with MGM. Yet, it seemed his success portraying a thug was simultaneously the beginning and end of his career. He was largely typecast as a one-dimensional villain thereafter. However, he did manage to turn this tough exterior into a rewarding role on the television series *Combat*, in which he played an army squadron leader in World War II. The show became a hit and earned Morrow an Emmy nomination. This success was likely an inspiration to one of his daughters, who would later forge an acting career of her own under the name Jennifer Jason Leigh.

Combat was canceled in 1967, and though Morrow found work on other projects, he continued to be cast as a tough-guy character and was increasingly anxious to gain some distance from these roles. There were TV spots here and there, but it was clear that he was getting older, and people were quick to forget his early successes. He struggled to find roles that would challenge him. Then, in the summer of 1982, he got the offer he'd been waiting for. For *Twilight Zone: The Movie*, Morrow was cast to play a bigot named Bill who had to confront his own prejudices as he was unwittingly swept through a series of historical events in which he was forced to embody the persecuted. In one scene, he is pursued by Nazis; in another he is the target of relentless white supremacists. His character pleads with his captors to recognize that he isn't who they claim he is, but his desperation goes unheeded, and he faces death repeatedly.

Warner Bros. had some reservations about the original script. The lead character was too one-dimensional, and the studio was concerned that audiences wouldn't relate to Bill's cold, racist personality. The general opinion was that the story would not serve much of a purpose without some form of redemption built into Bill's development. It was at the studio's urging that Landis decided to alter the events of the story. In one scene the script called for Bill to experience the horrors of the Vietnam War. The addition to the plot required Morrow to make a bold effort to save two young Vietnamese orphans from a small hut as a U.S. Army helicopter hovered above and destroyed their home. In the new scene, Morrow would traverse a shallow body of water as explosives ignited in the background while he carried the orphans to the shore, one under each arm. The seemingly harmless decision to imbue the segment with an inspirational note ultimately proved fatal to all three.

With Morrow now secured in the lead role, Landis and the production were tasked with casting two young children to play the orphans. Landis and the associate producer immediately saw a problem: The shoot was to take place at night, and state labor laws did not allow young children to work late hours. The laws also required any actor under the age of eighteen working on a film set to be accompanied by a state-certified teacher and welfare worker. These two restrictions limited their options for casting. It was suggested that two small dummies be used in lieu of actual children. The idea was quickly dismissed as an unreasonable compromise to the verisimilitude of the scene; it simply had to be real people. The restrictions against using children in this capacity were ignored as Landis pressed forward and continued to assemble the cast. Associate producer George Folsey Jr. began his search for two children, one boy and one girl about six to eight years old, who were Vietnamese, Chinese or Korean. He contacted Dr. Harold Schuman, the husband of a production secretary working on the film. Dr. Schuman was a psychiatrist who had recently acted as the director of a facility in South Central Los Angeles, a region that put him in close contact with the growing Asian population of the city. Folsey explained what Landis was looking for, though he neglected to mention that a helicopter would be used in the scene.

Dr. Schuman called a former colleague, Dr. Chen, who indicated that his own children were too old for the part. However, Chen contacted his brother and sister-in-law, who consented to allow their six-year-old daughter, Renee Chen, to participate in the project. Shortly after, Myca Dinh Le, the son of one of Chen's associates, was selected to play the other Vietnamese orphan.

Landis's cavalier attitude toward the law and safety became increasingly clear to those involved in production. Even Landis himself seemed to be aware of his blatant disregard for the law. Cynthia Gorney, reporting for the *Washington Post*, quoted a production secretary who testified in court that Landis was caught up with the grandeur of the upcoming helicopter scene, "Saying, you know, 'I want it big. I want it big.' And then he turned around and started up the hallway toward me. As we passed, he threw his arms up, and he said, 'Aargh, we are all going to go to jail.'"[14] Gorney reported, "'We decided to break the law,' Landis testified. 'I thought we would honor—if not the letter of the law, but the spirit of the law. I thought we would find children whose parents—we could explain to them that we were doing a technical violation. I understand that was wrong."[15] For almost any parent, the thrill of participating in a movie was too much to ignore, especially when that film had Spielberg's name attached to it, a strong asset after his recent internationally triumphant release of *E.T.* The agreement was for each child to receive $500 for one night of work.

To execute the scene, the production would also need a skilled helicopter pilot to negotiate the challenging maneuvers of a low hover amid explosions. One of their first choices was John Gamble, who held the position of chief helicopter pilot for CBS news in Los Angeles. The job didn't sound great to him: a diminutive fee for just one or possibly two nights of shooting. Also, his experience taught him that explosions such as the ones planned could lead to costly damages on a helicopter. In a prior incident, flying debris had damaged the router of his craft, resulting in $30,000 worth of repairs. Gamble eventually passed on the job, leaving the film without a pilot. On a tight budget such as this, costs were always a consideration and inexpensive resources were always explored. It was the pursuit of controlling costs that lead to Dorcey Wingo.

Though willing to work for less pay, Wingo was a thoroughly experienced helicopter pilot. *Twilight Zone: The Movie* was his first Hollywood studio feature, but there was no doubt that his numerous transport missions in Vietnam, as well as his thousands of logged hours, technical knowledge and professionalism, made him a very capable pilot. For Wingo, the proposition not only promised a paying job, but a rare opportunity to gain a foothold in the motion picture industry. The job came to him at a desperate time. His father-in-law had died at the age of forty, and in an instant, the man's young children were without financial support. Wingo stepped up and resolved to do everything he could to see that they would be looked after, but he couldn't meet even their most basic needs with his income prior to the picture. Wingo recalled, "It would have solved all my problems."[16] With a film credit like *Twilight Zone* to his name, he would have industry experience to point to while trying to make inroads in Hollywood. From a professional standpoint, accepting the job made a lot of sense. What bolstered his enthusiasm even more was the anticipation of working with Landis, a venerated director with an infectious spirit flowing from the exuberant cadence of his voice. He was a man who delved into discussions of the endearing B movies of his youth, old studio back lots rife with treasured props, and tales of inventiveness on shoestring budgets. His knowledge of film history can only be described as encyclopedic, as he effortlessly extolled the mastery of classic spaghetti westerns or delighted in the shamelessness of the tacky British movies of the 1970s. His thick beard, thin frame and saucer glasses gave him an avuncular look, but his hands gestured wildly as he conducted an orchestra of words, recalling the thrilling movies of his childhood. His innocent fascination with film makes it easy to imagine that part of him is still the eight-year-old boy enraptured with *The Seventh Voyage of Sinbad*.

The Last Shot of the Night

After waiting twenty-two years for another leading role in a feature film, Morrow was finally back where he wanted to be. At the age of fifty-three, he was starting all over. Many scenes in the script called for his character to brave several dangerous encounters, but Morrow, while mindful of safety, was willing to push himself further to accommodate Landis's penchant for realism at any cost. However, the scene to be filmed on the night of July 22 was something different, and it didn't feel right to Morrow.

The two young children, Myca and Renee, arrived on the set at 8:00 p.m. with ample time to prepare for their first shot, scheduled for 9:30 p.m. The cameras rolled as Morrow grabbed both children and rushed to the shore as an aquatic explosion jettisoned water and dirt into the air. The sound and debris frightened Renee, but the shot was achieved, and the children could all break before their next and final scene.

In the meantime, Landis and the crew set up to shoot another scene with Morrow at 11:30 p.m. The script called for him to stand near the river and scream to the hovering helicopter that he was an American and to stop firing at him. There was a notation on the call sheet mandating that a stunt man, Gary McLarty, double for Morrow in this scene, which involved heavy explosions. However, in the interest of authenticity, Landis insisted that Morrow perform the scene himself. McLarty was relegated to operating a machine gun aboard the helicopter, simulating an attack on the protagonist below. The cameras rolled and the special effects technicians on the ground ignited their explosives on cue. The immense rising fireball sent flames licking the helicopter and lit up the night sky. Sheets of water sprayed onto the windshield of the craft, obstructing Wingo's view and forcing him to stick his head outside of the cockpit in order to steer. As he came in for a landing, Wingo yelled, "They didn't tell me about this!"[17]

When he emerged from the helicopter, still feeling the heat of the explosion on his face, Wingo was furious. He approached the production manager and warned him about the dangers of allowing such incendiary power so close to the aircraft. They both knew there were more scenes to be filmed and more bombs to be detonated, and if Wingo was to continue, Landis and the technicians must be clear that any further events like this could be disastrous. Landis overheard Wingo's warning to the production manager. For such a freewheeling director, these torrid fireballs were nothing more than another color on his palette. Landis playfully boasted, "Well, that's just a warm-up for what's coming later."[18]

In anticipation for the next scene, a cursory inspection of the helicopter was conducted. The main rotor blade and the tail rotor blade appeared to be in good condition, indicating that the helicopter was still fully operational. There was still plenty of work to be done before the filming of the final shot at 2:00 a.m., most of which entailed putting back together what was destroyed in the previous scene. While the village was being reassembled, the rest of the crew broke for a late night meal, as required by the union. Landis and Paul Stewart, head of special effects on the production and a twenty-year veteran in the industry, surveyed the layout of the set and the locations of all the mortars to be detonated. Stewart had participated in preparations like this before; he held California's highest-ranking pyrotechnic license of the three levels recognized by the state. James Camomile, another special effects technician on the set, was the only other person with the same certification.

For Landis, the final scene had to be apocalyptic. As he and Stewart examined the mortars, the plan for the shot began to change. While pacing around the village, they arrived at a hut near the shore. The director remarked that he wanted to "see something happen in the shack."[19] Landis asked for an additional mortar to be placed within a hut resting near the shoreline. An eighteen-inch mortar, consisting of sawdust soaked in gasoline, was wired under the structure. This last-minute alteration was inconsistent with the previously agreed arrangements. The set had been prepared in such a way as to achieve the illusion that the huts were exploding from within. Each hut had been coated with a highly flammable paint that worked like a gelatinous fuel. The mortars were placed near the huts; no explosives were supposed to be placed inside them. When the explosives detonated, the flames would ignite the huts, causing the flammable paint to erupt in fire. The structure would have the appearance of exploding from the inside. But, with a fresh mortar wired from underneath, the hut by the shore would explode for real. Wingo had not been told about the change.

Later that night, Vic Morrow walked through the set, taking a mental note of where all the mortars were located. Landis followed along, and afterward, Morrow returned to his trailer to rest and await the final scene. His final review of the set likely did little to assuage his fears, which had begun even before he arrived on the set. Morrow had expressed his concerns about the haphazard production to his lawyer, Al Green, a few hours before departing for the shoot that night. Green indicated that Morrow wouldn't commit any contractual violations if he pulled out of the project. "I've got one more day to go and it will be behind me,"[20] Morrow replied. It was almost over.

Before the final scene, they conducted a brief rehearsal flight. Wingo ascended over the trees and made his way east toward the mock village. At approximately 1:30 a.m., Myca and Renee were gathered at their trailer and escorted to the makeup department. As 2:00 a.m. approached, one cameraman waited for the start of a pre-production meeting to review and discuss the placement of the explosives, but the meeting never took place. At 2:15 a.m., Landis, armed with a bullhorn, advised everyone to get in place. Over one hundred crew members and visitors stood ready for the last shot of the night.

James Camomile would fire off the explosives. Each bomb was connected to a wire running back to a series of copperplate contacts on his firing board. He completed the electric circuit to set off each bomb by running a tenpenny nail across the firing board. He protected himself with a welder's hood, shielding his eyes from any debris or dust kicked up by the helicopter. Others in the crew took similar measures to protect themselves. One technician covered himself with a furniture pad to guard against the heat, while the script supervisor put on a pair of safety goggles. Landis was positioned on a narrow peninsula that stretched out into the river, just east of the artificial village.

At approximately 2:18 a.m., Landis stood in the shallows of the river as he instructed filming to begin. Everyone was told to be on their feet in anticipation of the shockwave of the explosion. The helicopter lifted off and approached the position over the village. Landis shouted through his megaphone for the pilot to lower the hover. The helicopter dropped down to just twenty-five feet above the surface of the water and the actors below. Landis then gave his cue to the special effects technicians onboard the craft with Wingo. They provided simulated gunfire as another crew member, positioned on the peninsula, initiated the water squibs to provide the look of bullets hitting the water. Another crew member, armed with an air-powered marble gun, fired into the water near Morrow to complete the illusion of a barrage of gunfire.

Morrow picked up both children and made his way out of the hut onto a wooden pier. Once they reached the river, Camomile, on schedule, detonated three explosions at the edge of the village. Another technician set off explosions located to the left of the village. The force and heat of six mortars in just nine seconds was colossal. Two camera operators stationed at the top of a cliff, trying to capture the action, had to retreat amid the scalding heat and ash of the detonations. The first of the incendiary charges rolled off a nearby cliff, falling straight toward the helicopter. Dan Allingham, the production manager aboard the craft, shouted for the pilot to get away from the blast. Wingo tried to dodge the falling flames, but the explosions rising directly from below were overpowering. The craft faltered, and the fire began to envelop Wingo and the crew. The tail rotor suddenly ceased functioning. Without this stabilizing force the craft was nothing more than a piece of spiraling metal in the sky. Randy Robinson, a cameraman aboard the helicopter, recalled, "I could feel something was loose. We were spinning in circles."[21]

Morrow continued to make his way to the shore with both children, but his hold on Renee Chen loosened and she fell into the water. He reached out to pick her up just as the right skid of the helicopter descended upon her, crushing her to death. The spinning blade of the main rotor then crashed into the water, decapitating Morrow and Myca Dinh Le just a few feet from the shore.

The People v. John Landis

The National Transportation Safety Board concluded that "the probable cause of the accident was the detonation of debris-laden, high-temperature special effects explosions too near to a low flying helicopter leading to foreign object damage to one rotor blade." The excerpt continues with an assessment that "the proximity of the helicopter to the special effects explosions was due to the failure to establish direct communications and coordination between the pilot who was in command of the helicopter operation and the film director who was in charge of the filming operation." Buried within the technical analysis of the accident is a single phrase indicating the brevity of the disaster: "The examination included 228 frames of the film taken during an elapsed time of 9.5 seconds."

The California Occupational Safety and Health Administration (Cal/OSHA) also conducted an investigation. Their goal was to ascertain, through interviews, if all necessary precautions had been taken in preparation for the scene. The agency issued thirty-six safety violation citations against Levitsky Productions, Inc., John Landis, Western Helicopters, Warner Bros. and the Burbank Studios. After levying fines totaling $62,375, Cal/OSHA relinquished all files and evidence to the L.A. County district attorney, with a recommendation to pursue criminal prosecution on charges of manslaughter and violation of labor laws.

The funeral for Vic Morrow was held on Sunday, July 25. Landis was present, and even prepared a brief eulogy in which he made the bold and perplexing assertion, "Tragedy can strike in an instant, but film is immortal."[22] Two days later, Landis attended the funerals for Renee Chen and Myca Dinh Le. The film resumed shooting just a few weeks later, despite some discussion of shutting down the picture entirely, or perhaps just removing Landis's segment. However, the studio's decision about the outcome of the film was likely a minor concern in comparison to the variety of lawsuits filed in the wake of the incident. In August 1982, Mark and Shyan-Huei Chen pursued damages from all parties involved. In May of the following year, the Le family pressed forward with their own lawsuit. Wingo and Western Helicopters, Inc., also filed a lawsuit against Landis, Spielberg and Warner Bros., while one camera operator sued members of the production for injuries he sustained as a result of the crash. The suit issued by the children's parents against Landis would come to dominate industry headlines, while a much quieter suit initiated by Vic Morrow's daughters against Spielberg and Landis reached a settlement in November 1983 for an undisclosed sum.

Despite the disclosures made in the National Transportation Safety Board report, Landis regarded the early morning hours of July 23 differently. He remarked, "The idea of an accident is much too frightening for people. There must be someone at fault."[23] He offered his own assessment, explaining, "It took five years to figure out what had actually happened. When you read about the accident, they say we were blowing up huts—which we weren't—and that debris hit the tail rotor of the helicopter—which it didn't."[24] Landis later revealed that "the FBI Crime Lab, which was working for the prosecution, finally figured out that the tail rotor delaminated, which is why the pilot lost control. The Special FX man who made the mistake, by setting off a fireball at the wrong time, he was never charged."[25] Delamination occurs when the outer aluminum skin of the rotor blade separates due to heat exposure. Abdon Llorente, the chief investigator for the National Transportation Safety Board, would later amend his conclusion to indicate that one contributing factor in the crash may have been the delamination to which Landis was referring.

Four years passed between the accident and the commencement of the trial in which Landis faced two counts of manslaughter for the two children. He was also indicted on three additional counts of manslaughter through gross negligence. These grand jury indictments were disclosed the very same day as the release of *Twilight Zone: The Movie*, June 24, 1983. The final print, already tarnished by three deaths, was further discredited by a cacophony of criticism, describing the film as a vapid, unintelligent disservice to Rod Serling's legacy.

Los Angeles County deputy district attorney Lea Purwin D'Agostino was offered the position of prosecutor in the *Twilight Zone* case. Her incisiveness and unrelenting determination had led to a career full of courtroom victories, while her acrimonious style earned her the nickname "The Dragon Lady," a moniker first used by the defendant in the trial for the 1974 bombing at the L.A. International Airport. On the side of the defense was Nashville attorney James Neal, a name familiar to many who had seen his incandescent career take shape as a Watergate prosecutor in the 1970s, and as a leading force in the successful defense of the Ford Motor Company against charges of manslaughter in the Pinto case. Neal, like so many others, initially disliked Landis and his arrogant demeanor. Only after several meetings did he finally decide to accept the case.

As the trial date loomed closer, the lawyers and the judge spent nineteen days questioning a pool of 150 potential jurors. Ultimately, twelve were selected, a diverse mix of ethnicities. The group included a sixty-four-year-old retired army colonel, a budget analyst at the L.A. Department of Water and Power in his late thirties with two children, a secretary in her late fifties working for the L.A. Community College District, and a fifty-nine-year-old Louisiana-born machinist with four grandchildren. The trial was set to begin at the Criminal Courts Building in L.A. on September 3, 1986.

A small army of reporters set up camp in order to bring the trial to television, radio and newspapers across the country for the next ten months. Throughout the trial, bitter exchanges passed through the courtroom as the lawyers traded barbs. D'Agostino set the basis for her argument when she explained to jurors that the children were hired illegally in a deliberate attempt to eschew labor laws, and to conceal the danger she believed Landis and others were aware of regarding the explosives and the helicopter. Though the children *were* hired illegally, the defense would push forward the notion that the accident was unforeseeable and a result of a combination of exceptional circumstances beyond anyone's control.

In the end, the defense was successful. After thirty-two hours of deliberation over the course of nine days, the jury of seven men and five women reached a verdict of not guilty. Landis's wife wept as the court clerk read "not guilty" for every count of every charge against the defendants. D'Agostino only offered, "If we have succeeded in saving one life and deterring one director . . . then the prosecution was successful."[26] In his reflections of the trial, Spielberg explained, "This has been the most interesting year of my film career." He continued, "It has mixed the best, the success of *E.T.*, with the worst, the *Twilight Zone* tragedy. A mixture of ecstasy and grief. It's made me grow up a little more."[27]

The Directors Guild of America would later issue a vote of no confidence in regard to Landis's conduct, a measure which did little to slow his career, though he later expressed, "I relive the accident all the time."[28] Despite all his films, the deaths on the set of *Twilight Zone: The Movie* left an indelible mark on his life and career.

Recalling his attempts to toy with the ravenous media through-out the trial, Landis said, "In the courtroom, the camera was there all day just to get shots of me that they could use on the news. So, all day, whatever [the cameraman] did, I would just move my chair so I was always behind one of the lawyers."[29] In every environment, Landis remained the director of his surroundings, the final word in the mise-en-scène. He said, "There is a film rule that when you can't see the lens, the lens can't see you."[30]

2

Hollywood
Be Thy Name
Heaven's Gate

1,000 Rooms

WHY BUILD A PALACE that is impossible to inhabit? The only person likely to have an answer to that question has long been dead.

Nicolae Ceaușescu was destined to be the savior of his people. Born in Romania in 1918, he joined the ranks of the Romanian Communist Party at a young age. He eventually became its leader in 1965 and proclaimed his desire to bring Romania independence from Soviet political domination. To the people of Romania, he was a brilliant leader who seemed destined to awaken the country. Ceaușescu decisively ended Romania's cooperation in the Warsaw Pact and helped to cultivate a revered status with the United States and the British government.

A man with such a grand vision surely must have a grand palace, and so Ceaușescu held a competition inviting architects to submit design ideas for his future home. The winner was Anca Petrescu, a recent architecture school graduate. Her papier-mâché model captured the breadth of Ceaușescu's delusional mind with its impossible dimensions and boundless size. He mandated the destruction of nearly one-quarter of the city of

Bucharest to make room for the site of his new home—a shining, white monument to Ceauşescu's swelling dictatorship. The entire Uranus district was leveled, forcing out 40,000 residents, and the land was cleared to accommodate the Victory of Socialism Boulevard, a sprawling avenue reaching out from the palace like an outstretched tentacle. Not to be outdone, Ceauşescu mandated that the boulevard be wider than the Champs-Élysées.

A workforce of 20,000 men was recruited to begin construction of the mysterious palace. Three shifts were spread over twenty-four hours to ensure that the project continued without interruption for five years. Over 1,000 rooms were eventually constructed, lit with nearly 3,000 chandeliers that glowed with 700 light bulbs each, at a time when most Romanian homes were permitted only one sixty-watt bulb per room. In four hours the building consumed the same amount of electricity used to power all of Bucharest for a day. The palace leeched not only electricity from the country, but also vital natural resources. Ceauşescu insisted that the building be made entirely of raw materials from within the country; a total of 700 trainloads of marble were carried from Transylvania, leaving many Romanian cemeteries without sufficient resources for headstones. Acres of elm and oak trees were cut down, 550,000 tons of cement were mixed, and unending yards of carpet were sewn to adorn the dictator's ideal residence.

Ceauşescu and his wife visited the construction site for two hours every Saturday to speak with the workers about their progress. As the towering walls and distant ceilings took shape, it became evident that the project was the doomed illusion of a madman. Even Anca Petrescu, the chief architect, came to realize that her design had revealed the petulant indecisiveness of an unyielding man. She once lamented, "He was an impossible benefactor."[1] She continued, "We knew he was unable to gauge the effect of a column or a door if shown only a reduced model, so we had to build actual full-size papier-mâché models of columns or windows, and even then he was incapable of taking a decision." The inconsistent and unbalanced array of architectural styles within the palace echoes Anca's reflections and invites comparisons to the disparate appendages of Frankenstein's monster. The style has been described as rococo, Renaissance, baroque and Byzantine all in one. The dictator was once reported to have ordered the destruction of a sixty-foot-high marble staircase simply because the design was not to his liking.

The foundation of the palace sinks deep below the ground, with an enormous shelter sixty-five feet underground and a two-person railway specially equipped for Ceauşescu and his wife. Above ground, the structure is twelve stories tall and has a total floor space of over 300,000 square feet. The main reception hall is the size of a football field. Opulent details abound, including threads of gold and silver woven into the curtains. Yet, while the dictator and his wife labored over the exactness of these details, the people of Romania grew resentful of their oppressive ruler. People began to starve as Ceauşescu pumped nearly all of Romania's agricultural production out of the country in an attempt to repay heavy debts accrued from borrowing money from the West. Timisoara, the country's fourth-largest city, became the epicenter of the uprising that ultimately forced Ceauşescu and his wife to flee Romania. Their escape was unsuccessful, and on December 25, 1989, both were executed by firing squad.

The construction was halted, and for the first time in years the vacant marbled rooms and endless hallways lay in darkness and silence. The palace became an unforgivable reminder of the man who brought starvation and desolation to Romania. There were many controversies and disagreements concerning what could be done with the immovable relic, now called the Palace of the Parliament, with an interior only 60 percent complete. One government official summarized the ultimate predicament, "It would probably cost more to pull it down than to finish it."[2] There was no option but to surrender to the truth; there are some ravages that remain permanent.

This truth became a devastating reality to another group during the same decade of Ceauşescu's rule. A man named Michael Cimino was a rising talent in Hollywood, promising to bring a new era of filmmaking to the studio machine. Fresh from his Oscar-winning picture *The Deer Hunter* (1978), he arranged to make his next movie with United Artists. He called his script *Heaven's Gate*.

The production came to exhibit similar extravagances as seen during Ceauşescu's punishing administration. The budget almost immediately soared out of control, and the expenses of ego and frivolity began to reach insurmountable heights. Every desire of the director, no matter how frivolous, was to be met. He commanded control over all. The film became an exorbitant palace of its own as the feverish spending was outpaced only by its unending running time. Mismanagement and irresponsibility led to the collapse of the entire studio behind the film, and the very title *Heaven's Gate* came to inspire trepidation throughout Hollywood.

The Wild West

French film critic and theorist André Bazin once wrote, "The western is the only genre whose origins are almost identical with those of the cinema itself."[3] In his essay "The Western: or The American Film par Excellence," he regards this style of film as one that surpasses all others. For Bazin, "the American comedy has exhausted its resources," and "From *Underworld* (1927) to *Scarface* (1932), the gangster film had already completed the cycle of its growth." No other genre had the indomitable vitality of the western. "The western does not age," Bazin proclaimed.

How can this be? It is a genre seldom seen today in American film, and yet Bazin insisted, "The western must possess some greater secret than simply the secret of youthfulness. It must be a secret that somehow identifies it with the essence of cinema." If this analysis seems dated, it is likely because this essay was written several years before the ill-fated production of *Heaven's Gate* began in 1979, a year that in some ways marks the passing of the western from youthfulness to infirmity.

The script, originally known as *The Johnson County War*, was the work of Michael Cimino, who was also to be the director. He wrote the epic in 1971, when the grandeur of the western spectacle could never satiate an audience always anxious for more. As Bazin wrote, "[The western's] worldwide appeal is even more astonishing than its historical survival."

Cimino's script centered on three fictional characters in Wyoming at the beginning of the 1890s, during the Johnson County War. The war was the result of contentious turf disputes between European immigrants settling in the West and the cattle ranchers already established in the region. The bitter rivalry reached its pinnacle when the cattle ranchers hired mercenaries to kill the immigrants in retaliation for suspected theft of livestock. Cimino had already tried once to shoot the script before he was established in Hollywood or held any credits. These initial efforts were rebuffed by studios, given his then-unknown status in the industry.

But everything changed for Cimino after the success of *The Deer Hunter*, an affective story that follows a few young American men before, during and after their service in the Vietnam War. The brutality and poignancy of Cimino's examination of the devastating effects of war on the mind and body earned the respect of numerous Hollywood executives. In 1978 the film won five Academy Awards, including Best Picture, Best Direction, Best Sound, Best Editing and Best Supporting Actor for Christopher Walken. *The Deer Hunter* showed that Cimino was a man of considerable talents, a director who could deliver an emotionally charged and cogent story. Yet, just as Ceauşescu had to command that each room in his palace must be greater than the last, Cimino would have to exceed the now immense expectations of the audience and Hollywood. Much like Ceauşescu's young architect with her papier-mâché model, Cimino's vision began in a relatively modest form: a script.

As venerated screenwriter William Goldman wrote, "There is no picture without a script."[4] He continued, "No one knows what a film will cost until there is a screenplay. A screenplay is gold." It is likely that no one took this sentiment to heart as strongly as Cimino did when revisiting his script for *Heaven's Gate*. The sprawl of the Wyoming landscape, where the epic would take place, was matched only by the enormous span of the thirty-three-year narrative. While Cimino enjoyed his new reputation in Hollywood, his script was still a relic from the past and would require rewrites. The reasons for its rejection in previous years were still valid even after his recent success. It was criticized early on for lacking a sense of pacing and presenting an obscure narrative. Among the studio's trepidations was the growing fear that the era of the western was nearing its end. There were already signs that the viewing public was ready to move on from mountains and cowboys. *Comes a Horseman*, another western, was faltering at the box office while *Heaven's Gate* made its way toward production. So Cimino faced the task of erasing from the script any strong implications that the film was, in fact, a western.

The solution to this problem was to begin and end the movie with nonwestern elements. A prologue and epilogue were applied to the screenplay, giving extra dimension to the story and elucidating the origins and fates of the characters. The prologue originally represented only nine pages of the script, and the epilogue was barely one page. Despite such modest lengths, these two sections eventually came to represent potentially substantial budget overages and became a bartering chip for the studio when the deadline began to deteriorate. Whether the prologue and epilogue actually changed the perceived genre of the picture remains questionable. But this change succeeded in allaying the fears of United Artists executives and led to the accelerated progress of the production. This screenwriting sleight of hand has been performed by many writers in the past, including William Goldman. He recalled, "I wrote the first draft of *Butch Cassidy and the Sundance Kid* in 1965 and showed it to a few people, none of whom was interested. I rewrote it, really changing very little, and suddenly, for whatever reason, everyone went mad for it."[5]

As preproduction continued, Cimino selected Glacier National Park in Montana to be the predominant location for the shoot. In February 1979, a preliminary budget of $9.5 million was set; the shoot would last sixty-nine days. This supremely ambitious timeline targeted a Christmas release in 1979. These dates and numbers were almost immediately regarded with suspicion. Additional estimates anticipated at least a week or a week and a half of additional shooting time, which would increase the budget by roughly $1 million. Postproduction costs were predicted to reach $400,000 as a result of the accelerated Christmas deadline.

The Montana location presented its own challenges. Winter

snowfall posed an enormous risk to the safety and efficiency of the production, as the park roads were frequently closed in the winter as a result of heavy accumulation. Aljean Harmetz, a Hollywood executive who turned down the picture at an early stage, recalled, "I asked if he mightn't have a problem with snow drifts, and he said he was going to work around the weather."[6]

And the central problem remained: How does one reconcile the ambition of the screenplay with a budget that seems fit for a more modest production? The discrepancy perhaps said more about the scale of the production than it did about the initial cost estimates, which, for their day, were not small. The motion picture industry was, and remains, a business fraught with risk. Perhaps Cimino, with his stunning Oscar victories, reduced some of this risk with his presumably marketable name attached to the picture. Many have speculated that Cimino was dealing with issues of self-aggrandizement, yet it also seems true that the studio became equally enraptured with the young talent. The script, which had been dismissed in his earlier days, suddenly had a new glow. But, even those enthralled with the script were obliged to surrender to the unabashed truth of the numbers, and as with all feature motion pictures, the numbers were daunting.

Entertainment lawyer Peter J. Dekom explained, "Everyone knows that the motion picture business is risky; shirts that people have lost in this industry would easily fill the entire Sears retail chain."[7] In the 1992 edition of the article "Movies, Money, and Madness," Dekom revealed the cold facts behind the brutal returns of the movie business, warning that "the motion picture business generates internal rates of return of between 0% and 20% or more, with the average (and mean) somewhere in the 8%–15% area."[8] In the 2006 edition of the article, the numbers only became more intimidating, with "internal rates of return between

-20% and 20% or more, with the average (and mean) over the last five years somewhere in the -5% area." The sobering truth behind these numbers is the unique dilemma that a movie requires an enormous investment to be realized, and only when the picture is released will it be known if the product is truly marketable. Research on the market can be conducted and historical numbers can be evaluated, but just as a few slight changes to *Butch Cassidy and the Sundance Kid* turned a once ignored script into a treasure to the studios, those same minor changes during the creation of a film can have powerful effects on the outcome.

While the marketability and expected return on the film remained murky, the proposed budget wasn't much clearer. Cimino communicated to the studio that the budget for the picture would be $11,588,000, but this number didn't really represent the anticipated total. A ruling from the director mandated that any additional cost incurred in an attempt to meet the Christmas 1979 deadline would not be included in budget outlays. The single sentence in his correspondence to the studio gave Cimino carte blanche to spend in any way he saw fit, without having to absorb the penalties usually levied against a director who failed to adhere to an agreed budget. Steven Bach, former senior vice president of United Artists and head of its worldwide production, summarized the inescapable problem of this conditional statement, "What no one asked was: How do we differentiate between cost overruns designed to meet the Christmas release and cost overruns stemming from other causes?"[9] This arrangement established a professional climate in which Cimino was in control not only of the picture but also of the studio itself. It would later become clear that the odds of the budget remaining at $11,588,000 were as poor as the odds that they'd have a completed picture for the Christmas season.

Power Play

For all practical purposes, Cimino commanded a limitless budget, but his reach for power didn't end there. He collected $2,000 a week in expenses in addition to his $500,000 salary. He also retained the publication and editing rights, as well as the advertising approvals for the promotion of the film. Bach recalls one of the director's more avaricious demands that came in the form of a clause in his contract, stating, "Mr. Cimino's presentation credit shall be in the form 'Michael Cimino's "Heaven's Gate"' (or in such other forms as [Cimino] may designate); Mr. Cimino's name in such credit shall be presented in the same size as the title, including all artwork titles, and on a separate line above the title, and shall appear in the form just indicated on theater marquees."[10]

The final piece of the demand brings into question his grasp of reality, given that no studio is in a position to compel movie theaters to include the director's name on their marquees. These mounting stipulations evoke questions regarding how Cimino saw himself at the time. An interview with Nancy Griffin in the *Independent* gave some dimension to a man whose audacity is not without at least some justification. Cimino grew up on Long Island and graduated from Yale University with a master's degree in fine arts in 1963. Before long he was immersed in the high-profile world of advertising in New York City. Not one to be confined to the small screen of television commercials, Cimino relocated to the distant, sunny land of Hollywood with a heist movie he wrote titled *Thunderbolt and Lightfoot*. Clint Eastwood played the lead role under Cimino's direction. Four years passed before he embarked on *The Deer Hunter*, which came in over budget, escalating from $8 million to $15 million. Any questions about the vast budget overages could be directed to the row of Oscars his film snapped up.

The supreme confidence the director held in himself was only emboldened by his Academy Award victories. The recollections of those who have worked with him illustrate a regal image of the once unassailable auteur. In Griffin's article, former United Artists executive David Field recalled, "Michael had these people so spooked that no one dared to tell him to go shit in a hat."[11] It was likely that this power dynamic was also responsible for the right Cimino won to deliver a cut between two and three hours in length. He also managed to win a drawn-out dispute regarding the casting of the picture. Studio executives were eager to cast a more well-known actress in one of the lead female roles, like Diane Keaton or Jane Fonda, but Cimino insisted that Isabelle Huppert play the role of Ella Watson. This was only one of many arguments that would follow, but it set a dangerous precedent for the studio executives, who caved to Cimino's demands.

The decision had less to do with Huppert than it did Cimino. Bach, revisiting the decision, remembered, "The star of this picture—it was so clear—was Michael Cimino. We weren't betting that this or that actor or actress would add a million or two to the box office. We were betting that Cimino would deliver a blockbuster with 'Art' written all over it, a return to epic filmmaking and epic returns."[12] The decision to agree with Cimino's casting ultimatum was simultaneously a decision to press forward with the picture and to clear the way for more expensive power plays. Bach reflected, "Perhaps some less enlightened or more hotheaded production executives at another studio might have told Cimino to go fly a kite and thereby saved their company $40 million and its very existence."[13] Instead they gave him what he wanted because, "in what was perhaps the most naïve and seminal delusion of all, we believed that now that we knew Cimino's darker, colder side, we could better handle him in the future."[14]

In retrospect, this chain of concessions to Cimino was the ultimate undoing of the studio, but the decision to afford greater control to the director was not uncharacteristic of United Artists. In fact, it was an established practice of the company. Following World War II, studios struggled to remain profitable amid the dwindling audiences and escalating costs of production. The studios began to rely more and more heavily on valuable talent in order to establish audience loyalty and to float films with low production costs. This particular business climate precipitated a change in practices that marked both the beginning and the end of the United Artists studio.

In an examination of the history of United Artists, author Tino Balio summarized the decisive shift in strategy that put greater power into the hands of the talent. Balio explained, "To keep top producers and directors in tow, the majors formed semi-autonomous production units that offered the lure of creative authority in addition to a share of the profits."[15] The privilege of sharing in the profits of a picture could translate into big dollars for not only the director, but also in some cases a famous leading actor or actress who could secure the same deal. The system was devised to give greater control to the directors based on their previous successes. The more marketable the directors had proven themselves to be, the more autonomy they would be granted.

However, this response to the postwar decline in the film business generated other problems. Once their income became directly tied to the profits of the film, directors and actors entered the "management" stratosphere. While they make excellent artists, directors often exhibit lesser capabilities as executives, as seen in the extravagant spending on *Heaven's Gate*. As Balio wrote, the "flaw was that those traits of independence, flamboyance, and melodramatics that characterized the owners' work as artists could not be checked in the board room, severely handicapping the management of the company throughout much of its history."[16]

United Artists was founded in 1919 by the big stars themselves: D.W. Griffith, Mary Pickford, Douglas Fairbanks and Charlie Chaplin. The inclination to grant greater power to the actors is easily understood in a company that was started by actors. In the early days of United Artists, the company functioned only as a distributor of independent pictures. This small group of wildly successful actors had already reached the highest echelon of their profession and opted to circumvent the studio system in which they had once worked. They were no longer negotiating contracts; instead they were in a position to write them. They reigned over every conceivable aspect of their pictures, and this meant having to secure financing and accept greater financial risk while embarking on independent productions. This system gave the director not only creative control, but also a way of aligning their interests with those of the studio. Somewhere in the process of producing *Heaven's Gate*, however, this alignment disappeared. While director and studio wanted the best movie possible, there was undoubtedly a strong disagreement on how to achieve that goal.

Outlaw Inn

Preproduction began in Glacier National Park, but was abruptly halted after an avalanche. Several roads were shut down, including those used to access the shooting sites. Set building had to be suspended, which immediately vaporized the two-week padding built into the production schedule. The film was already two weeks behind schedule before production had even begun.

The Outlaw Inn is situated just off of Highway 93 in downtown Kalispell, Montana. The hotel, heavily trafficked by tourists to the national park, became the epicenter for the production. The principal cast and crew members occupied large blocks of rooms, including a portion of the top floor, which was converted into a makeshift production office. Floor space on the ground level became a hub for editing and film storage. Cimino's platoon turned the location into their base camp.

The first order of business was to build the enormous sets for the epic. The wild west of the late nineteenth century would have to be realized through careful construction and meticulous attention to historical detail. There was one set in particular that presented a laborious challenge. The script included an elaborate scene in which a large congregation of townspeople gathers for a dance. In the scene, the actors glide across a large wooden floor and pair off to dance—in roller skates. This slightly peculiar indoor set required no fewer than 300 construction workers. The scene later raised eyebrows among those questioning the historical accuracy of such a gathering. In the film's defense, Cimino remarked, "Roller skating did exist then. Those of us who worked on the film should know. We researched hundreds of photos from the period."[17] The appropriateness of the scene was an issue that some critics would broach long after the film was released. As construction continued, executives were already discovering budget overages that loomed in the distance. It became increasingly clear that the convergence of Cimino's monolithic vision, an endless script and production delays were going to cost the studio far more than originally planned. Rough projections indicated that United Artists could be looking at a $15 million project.

This vertigo-inducing amount put the studio on edge, but once again the booming echoes of Cimino's earlier success with

The Deer Hunter would prove to be a major factor in the decision-making process for *Heaven's Gate*. Eventually, the newly
approved budget found its resting place at approximately $11.5
million, yet the studio quietly resigned themselves to the overwhelming likelihood that the picture would not come in at a dime
under $15 million. The studio placed a heavy bet on Cimino, a
previous winner, hoping that after the spin of the wheel their
number would come up. The truth, however, is that past successes
do not guarantee future returns.

This discomforting fact became evident after the first six days
of shooting. Cimino was already five days behind schedule, but
the amount of exposed film he had gone through gave no indication of this. Sixty thousand feet of film stock had been used to
achieve only one minute and thirty seconds of footage that was
likely to see its way to the final cut. The cost of this effort was an
estimated $900,000. The once fearful prospect of spending $15
million soon became wishful thinking. Since it was a period
piece, the film was certain to accrue a dizzying array of future expenses. The *New York Times* reported that Cimino "hired 1,200
extras, each to be dressed in authentic period costumes. He
purchased a 19th century locomotive from Denver as well as
80 wagon teams. Everything about this epic was so epic that, as
one crew member quipped, he even 'interviewed 300 horses for
this movie.'"[18]

The news of production delays and eroding funds warranted
an immediate investigation into the practices surrounding the production. Any cost that could be reduced or done away with all
together would have to be targeted. The studio first learned of
the inefficiencies of the shooting logistics. Each day the crew had
to travel a total of four hours to and from location. This distance
consumed half of their eight-hour day. The construction of the

sets swallowed up an enormous portion of the budget, but it was later revealed that these sets were not just being built once, but rather several times. The verisimilitude of the set was a primary objective, regardless of labor and dollars. Another intractable issue was the decision to shoot and exhaustively reshoot many scenes, which indicated that the desired performance was elusive not only to the actors but to Cimino himself. Energy, time and money were wasted in the dogged pursuit of a vision that became more obscure with each successive take.

After the close of the second week of shooting, there was little to show for the directorial efforts of Cimino and for efforts of the studio to control costs. Thus far, a scant five-eighths of a script page had been completed each day; production was fifteen script pages behind where it needed to be. These diminutive achievements further exacerbated delays, placing the production ten days behind schedule after only twelve days of shooting. The disastrous beginning to the picture left some wondering what the future held for those already invested. Though the production was still in its early stages, enormous cash outlays had been committed. United Artists had already spent over $3 million to simply get the project off the ground.[19] They built a town on the shores of Two Medicine Lake in Glacier National Park; a nineteenth-century locomotive had been delivered to the set via a circuitous route designed to avoid tunnels, through which the train could not pass; vast sums had already been spent on the wagon teams; and hundreds of extras were provided with period clothing. And, of course, there was the roller rink. The greatest expense continued to be the lost time that accrued with every passing day. Cimino's fastidious attention to detail was not confined only to the set, costumes and props, but also to the tiniest nuances of each performance, and with each take came more film, more processing, and eventually more editing. Anyone entertaining the idea of abandoning the project would soon realize that the initial investments were far too substantial to be ignored.

Every bit of energy focused toward the authenticity of the film came at a cost. Cimino supposedly drove "20,000 miles in the state of Colorado alone during the six months he spent scouting locations."[20] The *Globe and Mail* quoted Cimino as saying, "Everything that appears in the film has a basis in a photograph of the period."[21] The entire town constructed for the film was "built on a platform three feet off the ground so as not to disturb the grass beneath it."[22] There was also the enormous cost of training all the actors and some crew members in skills like horseback riding, bull-whipping and how to drive a wagon. Perhaps these exhaustive methods used in the preproduction process were an early indication of the inefficiencies seen later during the far more taxing practice of shooting the film.

On average almost two hours of footage were captured per day, which amounted to less than two minutes of footage for the final cut. These modest gains cost the studio $200,000 a day. Out west, Cimino funneled a furious onslaught of bills toward the studio with seemingly little concern. In early June, when the filming was not even close to reaching the halfway mark, there were more than 600 names on the payroll. Approximately one month later, the number of employees rose to over 1,100.

One can't help but wonder if the region had some insulating effect on the project. Surrounded by the mountains and precise replicas of a past era, it may have been easier for one to forget the less metaphysical work of accountants back in Los Angeles. To a degree, the production was disconnected from the studio given this geographic distance. Not only did this lead to disjointed communication, but it also delayed bills and expense information from reaching the studio. Cimino seemed to believe that a film is a creature of its own, growing at its own pace to its own size and ultimately becoming a force that we must appease. In a *Newsweek* interview, he explained, "You're gambling with your life. How can you not have trouble making a film over a period of years? One reason is because you don't have the backup one used to have from the studio system—particularly doing period films. The inventory is no longer there. One starts from scratch now on everything. I had to go all over the world to find a man in Philadelphia to make top hats. No one wants to be over budget. But a movie is a living thing—everything begins growing. You have to go with that."[23]

While some were happy to continue feeding the beast that was *Heaven's Gate*, it became clear to the studio that something had to change. There were questions of spending, of logistics, of the schedule, and of a now long-gone hope for a Christmas release. Several weeks of photography had passed without the studio seeing any of the footage, but what they finally saw delighted them. The scenes indicated that at least some of the millions could be seen on the screen in the form of lavish production value. While the footage may have alleviated their initial frustrations, their questions remained unanswered and the dilemma was no less severe. The picture was far from complete, but with only a few weeks of shooting behind them, they had an inkling of the kind of financial damage this movie could do by the time it hit theaters, if it ever hit theaters. At the rate it was going, it could easily come in at several tens of millions over budget.

Studio executives needed to gain more control over Cimino, but this was not happening. Some began to question where the greater blame rested. Was Cimino merely a relentless spender, or was the studio unable to turn their resolve into action? Or did they simply miss their chance at producing a financially responsible picture from the very beginning? British filmmaker Michael Powell wrote about the *Heaven's Gate* production that "to turn a gifted amateur into a gifted professional, you need much discipline and control. Those just do not seem to be available in Hollywood anymore. To turn a gifted amateur loose is to guarantee disaster."[24] Powell then turned his attention to the shortcomings of some of the directors in this system, writing, "It reminds me of the decline and fall of the Roman Empire—an artist who'd insist on doing whatever he wants to do, no matter the limitations in money and time. After all, a person can tell his story with pen and paper, if he has to. These directors have as little consideration for the industry which they are ruining as for the bottoms of the public."

Further investigations into the spending on the picture reveal still greater wastes. For a battlefield scene, laborers undertook the expensive process of clearing the ground of rocks so that an irrigation system could be installed. The purpose of the irrigation was to promote the eventual growth of grass. They were literally watching the grass grow for a detail that would make very little difference to the audience come final cut.

As the expenditures rose, the crucial projection of box office receipts grew to impossible proportions. The standard formula is that a film must earn two-and-a- half to three times its cost in order to break even. It begins to turn a profit only after this amount has been reached. The final cost of the film was now estimated at $35 million, representing approximately three times the original budget of the movie. Just to break even in the theater, *Heaven's Gate* would have to earn close to $100 million.

The remaining options for the future of the picture were few, and all unpleasant. The studio could fire Cimino and bring in a replacement. They could shut the picture down entirely, or they could try to get him to speed up the production. Other studios were all too happy to decline requests to become partners on the film, which would have diluted at least some of United Artists' financial burden. The only option that allowed for even the slightest glimmer of hope was for the studio to state to Cimino in the most simple, straightforward terms that he must accelerate the pace of the production—for the sake of United Artists and for the sake of his own future in Hollywood. Cimino could no longer afford to shoot endless feet of film, like when he demanded fifty-three takes of actor Kris Kristofferson flourishing a whip. "That just about put me under, emotionally," Kristofferson recalled.[25] A new production schedule was drafted, and for any hope of survival it had to be strictly followed. There was no hope of coming in anywhere near the budget, and there was no hope for making the original release date. However, there was still hope—a silent, faint hope—for a good movie.

"Hollywood Be Thy Name"

The extent of Cimino's shooting on the set cannot be overstated. In the end, his western epic consumed nearly 1.5 million feet of film, and roughly 200,000 feet remained unprinted. All of this film represents 220 hours of viewing time—the equivalent of over one hundred feature-length movies. The mounting concern was whether or not there was even *one* good movie in that collection of raw celluloid. Film reviewer Vincent Canby wrote, "Much has been written and said about Mr. Cimino's 'arrogance' and 'self-indulgence' in taking upon himself the expenditure of whatever it was *Heaven's Gate* finally cost, while keeping the studio people away so that he might pursue the muse without interruptions.

Yet, no one would have worried about this if *Heaven's Gate* had turned into a hit. . . . Mr. Cimino's sin was that *Heaven's Gate* turned out to be a bad film."[26]

Cimino began to pick up speed on the set, but the studio was already beginning to feel the reverberations of bad publicity, some of which radiated out from the set itself. Freelance reporter Les Gapay made an initial attempt to interview the people attached to the film but was promptly turned away. He exchanged his interview request for the opportunity to actually work on the film. He was hired as an extra for the modest sum of $30 a day. The ground-level experience afforded him an intimate knowledge of the strife on location. Over the course of two months, he fulfilled his duties as an extra while taking notes and experiencing the exhaustion of endless working days. The former *Wall Street Journal* employee crafted just the story he set out for. The *Times* picked up the article, and it was eventually followed by a tidal wave of scathing articles about the inefficiency and extravagance of the production. Roger Ebert concluded, "This movie is $36 million thrown to the winds. It is the most scandalous cinematic waste I have ever seen."[27]

The painful chapter of principal photography finally came to an end on October 2, 1979. Then began the interminable task of crafting a visual story out of a length of film that could span the distance from Philadelphia to New York and back again. To release the movie within a year, the editing process would have to be continuous. Additionally, the prologue still remained to be shot while the editing took place. These first scenes took place at Harvard, but they were shot at Oxford, at the cost of additional millions. The New York release was scheduled for June 26, with a wider release contingent on the outcome of the premiere.

After the seemingly insurmountable difficulties, painful negotiations, logistical headaches and exhaustive power plays, the final cut—or what was originally thought to be the final cut—of Cimino's film was to be unveiled. Whatever was to adorn the screen in New York came at the cost of more than just dwindling studio dollars. The picture, like a rolling dust storm, would, in time, leave decimated relationships and careers in its trail. While the turmoil of making the film was a near endless journey, the viewing of the final product would be a similarly taxing experience, with a running time of five hours and twenty-five minutes. Of course, the film would have to be cut down to a more manageable length; after lasting only one week in the cinema, the movie was pulled from theaters to be reassembled for a nationwide rerelease. Reporter Geoff Pevere remembers the Canadian premiere of the film on November 19, 1980, where the bewilderment of the audience became uncomfortably clear. "At intermission, people surged toward the lobby in a collective desire to find ventilation and to ventilate. At the back of the University, the word 'disaster' hung in the air like the locomotive smoke we'd just seen drift across the widescreen vista of Wyoming."[28] American audiences, the few who saw it, were no more impressed. A particularly deleterious review by Vincent Canby asserted that the film "fails so completely that you might suspect Mr. Cimino sold his soul to the Devil to obtain the success of *The Deer Hunter*, and the Devil has just come around to collect."[29] However, leading man Kris Kristofferson stood by the film, remarking, "Everybody's heart was in it." It was undoubtedly a trying experience for him. "I remember sleeping in these little places, flypaper sticking to my face, and working 12 to 16 hours a day."[30]

The abridged reedit did little to resuscitate the picture. The devastation quickly spread beyond the scathing reviews and crippled relationships. The studio still faced the challenge of confronting a monumental financial loss. TransAmerica, the owner of United Artists, announced that it would lose a minimum of $29 million of its financing. The company established a pretax reserve to cover the losses of their total investment in the film, reported to be approximately $44 million. Executive Steven Bach, looking back on the events, summarized, "I don't hate Cimino, nor do I wish the movie ill: it would be like wishing ill of a corpse. But I felt so saddened by what had happened, because it was all for nothing. Nobody in Hollywood seems to have understood the most striking lesson of *Heaven's Gate*, which is that you can make a gigantic, expensive movie and nobody will come to see it."[31] In May 1981, TransAmerica accepted a buyout offer for United Artists from Kirk Kerkorian, the owner of MGM Film Company.

Bach knew it was time to make his exit. "My first sharp awareness that I had to get out of show business came on a shuttle flight from Washington to New York. Because my career required a great deal of flying, I had the habit on takeoffs and landings of reciting to myself the Lord's Prayer. . . . I stopped in mid-phrase, when I realized that what I had recited was 'Our Father, which art in Heaven, Hollywood be thy name.'"[32] He began teaching film studies at Columbia University. He was a man who, by all measures, loved movies, if not the movie business.

Michael Cimino's greatest critical success remains *The Deer Hunter*, a picture which well deserves its place in the annals of filmmaking. The story of *Heaven's Gate* echoed throughout the filmmaking industry, forcing other directors and executives to take notice of an imperfect system, and of just how damaging those imperfections can become. One executive remarked, "There is almost always something pleasing in the failure of a competitor, but *Heaven's Gate* is a catastrophe of such proportions that it's beyond laughing." Even Michael Eisner, then president of Paramount, admitted, "Our economic pattern is insanity, total out-and-out, unmitigated, predetermined insanity."[33]

3

King of
the Moon
*The Adventures of
Baron Munchausen*

Lies

EVERYONE WANTS ONE good story to tell, and any audience's enjoyment of a story hinges not only on the events recounted, but also on the artistry of the telling. Stories are not just subject to the occasional omissions of our memories, but to the additions made by our imaginations in an attempt to hold the attention of others or perhaps fill a gap or two. Therein lies a problem, that one lie begets another.

Consider the story of Stephen Glass. In 1995, a year after graduating from the University of Pennsylvania, Glass began his career in journalism as an intern at the *New Republic*. By the age of twenty-five, he was an associate editor. Though his peers described him as insecure, the boy wonder managed to regularly adorn the pages of the magazine with fascinating and original investigative articles. Glass was always the first to report on bizarre, incredible events, and he was also the last; it seemed no one was able to contact his sources. [1]

Glass's deception began with small lies. He started to fabricate quotes when his articles needed an extra punch to hold together. When the fact checkers and editors at the *New Republic* examined his sources, he went to extravagant lengths to fabricate their

existence. Soon he began to make up entire articles. His expand-
ing universe of lies included fake letterhead, fake voicemail and
even fake mistakes for the editors to catch and correct, so as to not
make Glass appear *too* perfect.[2] After everything unraveled, it was
discovered that twenty-seven of the forty-one pieces he wrote for
the magazine during his tenure were partially, or in some cases
completely, fictitious.[3] He later recalled, "When the first few fab-
ricated stories were done and fact-checked and the articles were
turned in, my editors loved them; more than that, they loved
me—I felt it."[4]

Glass was just doing what we humans love to do: telling stories. As the playwright David Mamet observed, "Storytelling is
like sex. We all do it naturally. Some of us are better at it than others."[5] Though Glass did it for esteem, many of us do it to entertain
or to be entertained, and sometimes we do it to get what we want.
Mamet continued, "Talking a potential partner into bed, a boss
into a raise, a supplier into a discount—each of these is a drama."
Perhaps this is why some who encounter a particularly fantastic
story will often put their own doubts to rest with the simple notion
that it doesn't even matter whether it's true or not, since it makes
for a good story either way.

One man who undoubtedly held this belief was Karl Friedrich
Hieronymus von Munchausen, otherwise known as Baron Munchausen, or "the baron of lies." Both a historical and literary character, the baron was known for the tales of his wild adventures.
Born in Germany in 1720, he served as a cadet in the military
before ascending to the rank of lieutenant in the Russian army in
1740. He fought in two campaigns against the Turkish army
before retiring to his patrimonial estate in 1760. In his later years
he began to share stories of his strangest, most harrowing days.
As noted in the introduction of Rudolph Erich Raspe's *The*

Surprising Adventures of Baron Munchausen, his tales were "embellished with palpably extravagant lies as to crack with a humor that was all their own."

In 1987, 190 years after Munchausen's death, Terry Gilliam, another man intrigued with the fantastic, tried to bring the baron to life on the screen. Whereas Munchausen was able to let his dangerous escapades unfurl in the safety of his imagination, Gilliam would face a far more real journey into an interminable hell. From the first day of production, the making of the film came to resemble the quixotic and surreal events of the baron's imagination, though for the director, studio, cast and crew, the ending was unwritten and always out of reach.

Box Office Bandit

In 1981 Terry Gilliam was one of the most sought-after directors in Hollywood. His third directorial effort, a childhood adventure titled *Time Bandits*, was a $5 million production that brought in $40 million in ticket sales alone. To many, this enigmatic director must have seemed like an overnight success, but his journey had begun decades before in his home state of Minnesota.

Though he appeared to be the first in his family to pursue a career in film, Gilliam learned later in life that his grandfather had run a cinema in Bismarck, North Dakota. "It seems very strange that from that far back there was a connection with movies, except I didn't know about it."[6] Gilliam's ultimate goal was more audacious than to own a theater; he wanted to tell his stories on the screen, and he had many to tell. The country setting of his childhood nurtured his sprawling imagination. As a boy, he often spent his days at a local swamp where discarded logs lay in huge piles. He would crawl through the cavernous openings and explore his own world. He devoured Robert Louis Stevenson, Hans Christian Andersen and countless comic books. In his reflections on an ordinary upbringing, Gilliam remarked, "I wasn't poor, I wasn't black, I wasn't blind, I wasn't anything. I said, 'I don't have a chance in the creative world.'"[7] He believed he had to suffer if he was to become a serious artist. "That's why I worked so hard on my schizophrenia," he joked.[8]

Gilliam's path to filmmaking was as circuitous as the plots and adventures that eventually formed the core of his work. As a young man he believed that his true calling was to become a missionary. Later he enrolled in Occidental College as a physics major. Soon after that, he directed his focus to political science and eventually joined the campus humor magazine, where he worked as a photographer, writer and cartoonist, which was perhaps his favorite experience and that which brought Gilliam into the world of filmmaking.

After a stint as a television animator, Gilliam found his place as the lone American in the troupe of comedic misfits that formed Monty Python. He created short stop-motion vignettes that came to life from carefully arranged cutout images. In this two-dimensional world, Gilliam told his stories with the agility and dexterity of a marionette puppeteer. Gilliam's feature directorial debut came with *Monty Python and the Holy Grail* (1975), codirected by Terry Jones. Just six years later, *Time Bandits* was released, and Gilliam enjoyed enormous success. "For a period there I was hot. I had suddenly been elevated to a hot director."[9] Though many offers were made, he had no interest in the Hollywood scripts that came to his attention. Instead he set his sights on a film called *Brazil*, the story of a man's search for his soul amid a futuristic dystopia. Postproduction, though, turned into a power struggle with MCA president Sid Sheinberg after Gilliam delivered the final cut to Universal with a running time eleven minutes longer than contracted. In an effort to bring more visibility to the studio's reluctance to release the movie, Gilliam took a whole-page ad in *Variety* which read, "Dear Sid Sheinberg: When are you going to release my film *BRAZIL*? Terry Gilliam." The letter forced Sheinberg's hand and eventually led to the release of the 132-minute director's cut.

Though battered and bruised, Gilliam had come out on top once again. He had done the impossible; he had built a box office hit with *Time Bandits* and had made a film all his own after wresting *Brazil* from the hands of unyielding studio executives. With two successes to his name, he seemed poised for a hat trick. Yet, just as one lie begets another, his next film was to be bigger and more extravagant than the last. No spectacle would be spared for his next tale.

The idea for *Munchausen* began to take shape during a visit to the home of ex-Beatle George Harrison during the summer of 1979. Harrison showed Gilliam a leather-bound publication of Raspe's *The Surprising Adventures of Baron Munchausen*, first published in 1785. Though lesser known in America, the amazing journeys of Munchausen have been bedtime stories for generations of German children. The telling of monolithic sea creatures and trips to the moon brought surreal dreams to the children who listened in delight. The stories fascinated Gilliam, and the book's illustrations by the French painter Gustave Doré captured his imagination. "In many ways it was the Doré illustrations that seduced me," he remembered.[10]

Once again, a Terry Gilliam project splashed across the pages of *Variety*. This time, however, the mood was triumphant and joyous. After a deal had been struck with 20th Century Fox for financing *The Adventures of Baron Munchausen*, a four-page advertisement in *Variety* exploded with superlatives announcing the project as "the world's biggest, most outrageous, mostest film."[11] It seemed nothing could curb the instant enthusiasm for what was slated to become the capstone of Gilliam's sublime career.

Do As the Romans Do

Arnon Milchan, the producer behind *Brazil*, orchestrated the *Munchausen* agreement with Fox. The arrangement was swift and amicable, and the contract was dashed off with the same childlike exuberance promised by Gilliam's new screenplay of magic and wonder. However, production problems began immediately, and they can be traced back to a single piece of legalese buried within the contract. A section called the "key man" clause mandated that various members of the management at Fox be designated as "key" players in the arrangement. When several of these executives left their positions at the studio, the contract was rendered invalid. The new Fox CEO, Barry Diller, had no interest in the esoteric project and dismissed the production almost immediately.

Gilliam later discovered that Arnon had been given $150,000 from Fox to finance some of the initial preproduction of the film. "It was the first I ever heard of it," Gilliam said. "I'd never seen a penny of the advance."[12] With the contract null and void, Fox insisted that the money be returned. This unpleasant revelation of withheld funds resulted in Arnon's departure from the film and a rift in his relationship with Gilliam that would last for six years. Only a short time after the declaration in *Variety* promising an unmissable film, the director lost his studio and his producer. New financing for the picture was eventually found at Columbia, where a deal was struck for a "negative pick-up." The studio would pay $20.5 million upon completion of the film in exchange for rights to the worldwide theatrical release and video sales. However, Columbia was uncomfortably familiar with Gilliam's earlier financial troubles with *Brazil* and *Jabberwocky*, Gilliam's first picture as sole director. As a result, a film completion guarantor was needed, and the bonding company Film Finances agreed to fill this role. In the event that the picture ran over budget or beyond schedule, Film Finances would step in to provide the additional funds necessary to complete the film. With this system in place, Columbia had assurance that they would not face any unforeseen expenses. The bond from Film Finances came at the cost of $1 million and an additional $2 million contingency fund for potential unknown future expenses.

Despite Columbia's promise to pay on delivery, the budget was a fraction of what would be needed to helm a production with the epic battles, moon adventures and ocean voyages that were tucked inside the pages of the script. The proposed solution was encapsulated in one simple word: Rome. Gilliam and others believed the cost of making the picture in Europe would be 30 to 40 percent less expensive than in the United States. Gilliam later admitted that the film could have been made much cheaper in England. In an attempt to adhere to their limited budget, the newly hired German producer Thomas Schühly found an accountant to assemble a detailed financial plan. The first effort indicated the film could be completed at a cost of $60 million. The accountant was promptly fired and replaced with another, who came up with a figure of $40 million; he was also fired. Finally, a third accountant was brought on and managed to squeeze the numbers enough to fit their budget. Sometime later, this accountant was also fired.

Soon the whole production team was off to Cinecittà Studios in Rome, which became the home for *The Adventures of Baron Munchausen*. As Gilliam began his preproduction, Schühly was busy galvanizing the local press with descriptions of a beautiful and magnificent forthcoming movie. The press was happy to share his excitement, calling Gilliam's project "Un Kolossal." Yet, filming was only a few weeks away and it seemed nothing was adequately planned. The uneasiness of a fast approaching shoot exacerbated tensions between director and producer. "As far as I was concerned the organization of the production was rat shit from the start. Thomas constantly assured me the way you worked in Italy was different. You saw nothing at first, then it all happened."[13] The truth was much different. Gilliam and production designer Dante Ferretti spent months scouting locations for shooting. After securing a location, an entire scene would be meticulously planned for the area, including measurements for sets, lighting designs and camera tracks. One such location was the Alhambra, a stunning Moorish palace in Andalusia, Spain, with towering ceilings and enormous, stately gardens. Just one month before filming a pivotal scene within the palace walls, Gilliam and the entire crew were told no camera tracks could be used, no smoke was permitted, and no horses may enter. All of the most important components of the scene were prohibited without any advance warning.

The disappointment with the Alhambra was just one of many last-minute collapses in shooting. Gilliam remembered, "This business of finding locations, spending months designing what we were going to do there, and then at the end be[ing] told we can't get the location. This happened probably four or five times in the course of the preparation."[14] He continued, "You'd say, 'OK, we're going to shoot this scene in this location.' And they'd say, 'No problem.' And then you'd spend a couple of months designing and preparing, all for that location. And then after these couple of months, somebody would say, 'Oh, we can't get permission.' So you start all over again. We remade the film several times before we even started shooting."[15] The frustrations between Gilliam and his producer worsened. Schühly ignored critical meetings meant to address the growing problems of the production, and many crew members had not been paid for weeks. Meanwhile, Schühly was increasingly inaccessible and spent most of his time trying unsuccessfully to bring Marlon Brando into the production in an effort to gild the cast list. At Gilliam's urging, Schühly was finally forced to abandon his pursuit of Marlon Brando. Gilliam recalled, "I remember when Brando sent his telex saying, 'Thanks, but no thanks.' Thomas just looked at it and said, 'He doesn't mean it.' I said, 'Yes, he does. It's right there.' It was incredible. The whole film was in danger of not being prepared, and he still thinks he's got a chance to get Brando."[16]

When Schühly redirected his focus to the production he became aware of the mounting problems for *Munchausen* and resorted to his own unique style to combat the issues. Like a town crier, he made daily announcements to the press about the enormity of the production that promised to be the biggest spectacle ever put to the screen. Taking him at his word, opportunistic locals seized a chance at quick income. Many bit players hired for nothing more than a walk-on were commanding unheard-of salaries; some even posed as production assistants claiming $2,000 a week. Italian drivers asked for $1,000 a week and often arrived in their family car. While driving cast and crew to and from the set for ehearsals they would often stop at an auto shop to have long overdue repairs made, all of which came at the expense of the production.

The new start date was set for September 7, and as it began to loom many of the costumes and sets had still not been completed. With a period piece like *Munchausen* every thread of fabric and stick of furniture had to be painstakingly re-created to match the era of the narrative. The first days of shooting called for the completion of a bombed-out theater, but unpredictable weather impeded the construction, as the set was located inside a studio that itself was without a roof ever since being decimated in World War II.

With every setback came escalating expenses. It cost more to fix the set, more to complete the costumes, and above all, it cost more as the most precious of all commodities began to erode: time. As a result of numerous delays, the cast, crew and all their services reached a total of $700,000 a week.

Over 6,000 miles away, back in Los Angeles, Gilliam's nightmare was scarcely acknowledged. Studio executives still maintained their early enthusiasm for the project, knowing little of the disasters that had ensued before even a single foot of film had been shot. One financier called Cinecittà Studios the night of September 7 to inquire about how the first day of shooting had gone. The response from Schühly was deflating; he explained nothing had been filmed for the day. The date for commencement of principal photography had been pushed back once again, and now the film was set to begin shooting on September 14.

The financier's surprise over this news was indicative of the lack of communication on the set. Often the misunderstandings between British and Italian crew members protracted the expected completion time of on-set tasks. In the meantime, many of the actors were left with empty days, again at a cost to the production. When actor and ex–Monty Python member Eric Idle arrived from France to film his scenes, he discovered there was little for him to do, leaving him wondering why no one had called to tell him of schedule changes before he left.

For some it was a matter of waiting; for others there was never enough time, until one day when an accident on the theater set

brought everyone some welcome relief. A portion of the scaffold-
ing collapsed onto the structure, ruining much of the set. No one
was injured, and the accident insurance would help to cover the
cost of a lost week, giving those in the costume department a few
desperately needed days to catch up. The accident was so perfectly timed that some began to whisper about sabotage. The net
result was yet another week tacked onto the swelling preproduction schedule that jettisoned the shoot to a distant, unreachable
horizon. The start date was moved once more, to September 21,
and the assembled actors would have to wait longer.

For every stroke of good luck, there seemed an unending
string of new problems. The script called for the baron's horse to
perform a repertoire of stunts, but the four horses that had been
tirelessly trained for months were struck with African horse fever
and placed into quarantine. Then there came the news that two
dogs, Argus I and Argus II, also trained to perform, were debili-
tated by a liver ailment.

Next, at the worst possible moment, Columbia chair and CEO
David Puttnam resigned, which put the fate of the troubled *Munchausen* film in the hands of an uneasy group of executives eager
to disown a production that was all but certain to fail. Without a
single frame of film exposed, the picture now stood at $2 million
over budget. This brought another player into the financial drama
of the project: the insurance giant Lloyd's of London. When Film
Finances had agreed to act as a bonding company for the film,
they streamed much of their risk to Lloyd's, which agreed to meet
any costs that exceeded $2 million above the budget. At this point
the London firm faced the strong likelihood that they would have
to provide funding all the way to $8 million over budget. Any fur-
ther costs above the once unimaginable $10 million mark would
revert back to Film Finances. One investment banker remarked,

"When the ship goes down, they ring a bell at Lloyd's."[17] The impending financial burden threatened to be a crippling blow to Film Finances, which began to wonder if Columbia would deliver on its promise to pay $20.5 million if the film was completed.

The Terry Gilliam that most were accustomed to seeing on set had become a distant memory. Often sporting a straw fedora with a twisted brim, he once watched in delight as the actors took great care to indulge in the fantastic vernacular and events of the baron's outlandish life. "Your reality, sir, is lies and balderdash and I'm delighted to say that I have no grasp of it whatsoever."[18] His laugh is unmistakable, an ebullient hiss that gives way to a high-pitched, childlike giggle. However, this shared exuberance during rehearsals and early meetings was now a faint echo. Frequent disasters had caused a tectonic shift among the production staff, and their doubts and troubles cast a heavy shadow over their work. Furthermore, the literal shadows that hung above the roofless Cinecittà studio often drenched the crew at night, while the punishing heat during the day sometimes made shooting impossible. Yet, director, producer, cast and crew pressed on; there was no other option.

Due to the troublesome weather, many scenes were rescheduled to shoot in Spain. This meant not only that cast and crew had to be relocated to a different country, but also that the equipment and costumes would have to be taken abroad. This additional level of logistics led to an unprecedented occurrence of lost luggage. Upon boarding a plane for his ultimate destination of Almería, Gilliam was dismayed by the enormous heaps of baggage being loaded onto the aircraft. In genuine concern for the burdensome weight of these suitcases, he wondered how the pilots could ever lift off the runway. He was assured however, that many pieces were to be left behind in consideration of maximum weight limits.

Sadly, those items discarded on the runway included most of the costumes for the production, among them 400 Turkish soldier outfits. These essential components of the scene would be shipped over on the following flight, as the limited cargo space on the first departure had to be reserved for the Italians' personal wardrobe. In the end, the costumes finally touched down in Barcelona, hundreds of miles away amid a customs strike at the airport, only to be relinquished after the greasing of a few bureaucratic palms.

Gilliam, now having to adopt the role of a pugilist quite frequently, witnessed another adversary enter the ring in the form of a sixty-three-year-old man named Allan Buckhantz. Buckhantz claimed to hold remake rights to a 1943 film version of the Munchausen tale titled *Die Abenteuer Des Baron Munchausen*. His evidence of ownership was a 218-page script in addition to over 3,000 production illustrations and a detailed budget drafted in preparation for his proposal to Columbia. Buckhantz took issue with the fact that his proposal had been turned down by the studio in 1987, only to be given to Gilliam three months later. Columbia asserted the story of Munchausen was part of the public domain and without copyright protection. The lawyer representing Buckhantz insisted that if Gilliam's final picture—should it ever see the light of day—contained any concrete similarities to the 1943 version, the studio would be faced with a copyright infringement lawsuit. With millions already behind Gilliam's picture, the studio was left with only one option: to press forward and hope the already volatile situation with the lawyers would never reach critical mass.

In the meantime, all cast and crew remained focused on achieving the seemingly modest goal of shooting the first scene of the production. One popular measure of speed and productivity on a shoot is the number of "set-ups" completed per day. A set-up is the act of positioning one camera in one location and adjusting the lighting to accommodate a single shot. Most scenes are filmed from several angles and thus require numerous set-ups. After endless days of preparation and struggle the cast and crew of *Munchausen* finally completed their first set-up. A bottle of champagne erupted with the gusto of an ecstatic crew anxious to see the preproduction come to an end. But they had no idea of the sleepless nights that lay ahead as shooting began.

A Moon without a King

Ambition and fierce attention to detail have long been the pride and perilousness of any Gilliam production. During one summer while he was in college, Gilliam worked as a drama coach at a theater camp for children and led them in a production of *Alice in Wonderland*. Six weeks of preparation would culminate with a single performance on Parents' Day, when students would demonstrate an entire summer's worth of skills developed under the strict tutelage of their instructor. Only one short week from the day of the show, Gilliam still felt the production was inadequate and disorganized. His course of action to avoid failure was decisive and simple: Cancel the entire event. But the play was slated to be the central achievement of the summer for the young actors, and this impromptu decision let loose a flood of angry responses from the campers and their parents.

This inexorable memory likely became even more vivid as difficulties with *Munchausen* continued to escalate. At this early stage, communication had nearly shut down between the Italians and the Brits working in Rome. Meanwhile, the unit shooting in Spain moved at a glacial pace, yielding a mere thirteen minutes of exposed film during the course of fourteen days. As a result of a delayed start and slow progress, the swelling budget brought the financing of the picture into question. After a failed attempt to solicit further money from Columbia, the movie seemed to be on perpetual life support. On August 15, 1987, the budget stood at more than $23 million; less than two months later, on October 11, the revised budget had ascended to $32.9 million with little to show for the increased cost. In a bold move, Film Finances stepped in to take over the production. Shortly afterward they issued a communiqué to the crew and staff of the film, declaring that as of November 7, 1987, their contracts were terminated. The project was officially shut down without any indication of when, or if, shooting would resume.

This halt was designed to give the bonding and production companies time to tackle the multitude of financial problems plaguing the film. Film Finances held to the notion that firing Gilliam and replacing him with another director might return the film to the terra firma of financial stability. Gilliam saw the move coming: "They're trying to fire me, there's no question about that. They say they have two directors waiting in the wings."[19] However, this proposal was short-lived, as it became clear that the initial contract with Columbia was specifically for a Terry Gilliam film. If another director were to command the production, the studio would no longer be purchasing a product of Gilliam's efforts and would not fulfill their contractual obligations. Gilliam's cavalier attitude toward the threat of losing his job was reflected in his simple assessment of the situation: "I was hoping they would!" he admitted. "Please pull the plug! Fire me! There were threats I was going to be replaced which was nonsensical, because any half-way decent director would have taken one look, and turned around and gone straight back again."[20] It was clear that losing Gilliam was not the solution.

Instead, Plan B was initiated. This new protocol was more painful than the threat of termination. Film Finances called for the reduction and elimination of various pages of the script to save on production costs. The project, now hemorrhaging money, would have to lose some of its parts to save the whole. One scene in the 126-page script that was to be immediately amputated was the spectacle of the baron's amazing journey to the moon. The scene called for the baron and his boat to be swept away to the lunar surface during a cataclysmic and fantastic ocean storm. Originally, the baron was to discover a plethora of inhabitants on the moon played by nearly 2,000 extras. Though Gilliam and cowriter Charles McKeown hated the idea of sacrificing the moon sequence, they saw no other way to stave off the furious onslaught of accountants and lawyers banging at the gates. Yet, before relinquishing the entire episode, another idea was proposed. "Look, Terry, let's at least de-populate the bloody moon," McKeown begrudgingly suggested.[21] But the proposal to diminish the scene's cast of 2,000 to a mere two seemed laughable, and Gilliam responded with intense frustration. "Let's just tear the shit out of the whole thing. We'll shoot the entire episode in my office! Everyone can just sit around in their costumes and read the script. That'll make it really cheap."[22]

Cuts to the script and shrinking the moon sequence did little to appease the fury of Film Finances. The smoldering relations between director and financier worsened when Sean Connery, originally cast as the king of the moon, dropped out of the picture after learning of the drastic cuts that had been made to the scene. Film Finances disliked the notion of a big name making an exit from the film because it would leave them with one less card to play when the time came to promote the picture. A mutually disastrous impasse seemed inevitable, and the conflict turned personal. It has been reported that while facing astronomical losses, Film Finances threatened to seize Gilliam's assets to recoup the budget overages. One possession that came into their crosshairs was Gilliam's home, known to locals as Old Hall, a three-story house north of London and once the dwelling of Sir Francis Bacon. A stroll through the interior reveals a tangible manifestation of Gilliam's fertile imagination. The ceiling of the master bedroom is painted to look like a blue sky dotted with clouds, and some rooms feature stained glass windows salvaged from a demolished church. He also keeps a collection of props from his earlier films *Time Bandits* and *Brazil*, now distant echoes of a career that once seemed to be on course for unmitigated success.

These threats that involved Gilliam's personal life and assets awoke a rage within. "My wife was pregnant at the time, you go a bit crazy when this starts happening."[23] Furious, Gilliam had to be removed from the conference room where the meeting was being held. While pacing through a parking lot, he turned to the nearest car and pounded his fist against the windshield, shattering it to pieces. Pausing to assess the blunt force of his wrath, he realized that it was his own car that he had hit. The following weeks he would be seen driving behind the wheel of a car with no windshield. The personal war had undeniably galvanized the distraught director, and his rage provided endless fuel for the rigors of that night's shooting, which proved to be the most productive and successful of the entire production. This became a common theme on the set. Gilliam recalls participating in "crisis meetings where we've got forty-eight hours to come up with the answer, and thirty-six hours later there's no answer. So, that's it! Call the lawyers, it's all over, the film is dead, the Baron is finally buried. And then, Bingo! At the last minute we've found an answer every time. I have never seen a film so determined to keep going."[24]

One particularly inspiring event was the shooting of the hot-air-balloon scene. In an ingenious escape, the baron charms the local women to give up articles of their clothing which he sews together into a makeshift hot-air balloon. The filming of the scene posited the unique problem of inflating a real balloon beneath a shell of women's garments. The baron's balloon would not ascend properly under the constant gusts of wind on the outdoor set. Eventually, the crew resorted to attaching the floating structure to a crane and lifting it artificially. Yet, the unyielding winds still prevented them from getting the shot they needed. With daylight fading, it seemed impossible that the shot would be made that day; the baron would never make his escape. Then, once again, a benevolent force took hold. "With only an hour or two of daylight left the sky cleared and the wind dropped," Gilliam recalled. "Just then the sun broke through, the balloon turned and we got the perfect shot."[25]

This sliver of good fortune would once again provide a meager respite from the problems when it came time to recast the role of king of the moon. The director and financiers were already nervous about the prospect of a picture without an actor as recognizable as Sean Connery. Plenty of negative publicity already threatened to overshadow the release, as distant as that goal seemed. As the eleventh hour drew near, cast member Eric Idle reached out to friend Robin Williams, who was delighted to lend his madness to the film as the character of the moon king. But Williams, lacking trust in the producer Schühly, insisted that his name never appear in the credits of the film and that he never be included in publicity photos. If his name was attached to the doomed project he would likely become the single asset leveraged in forthcoming efforts to court audiences and promote the picture, leaving Williams uncomfortably linked to a dismal film.

Gilliam later recalled that Williams's lawyers "thought we were going to just use his name to salvage the movie, so we had to agree to eliminate him from the publicity campaign. There was a phrase they kept using. They didn't want us, quote, 'to pimp his ass to save our picture.'"[26] Relinquishing the right to promote Robin Williams as a cast member was a small concession for his explosive persona in the role of the king. For a brief time, both the artistic and financial ends of the production were content. However, the calm was all too brief.

As feared, Allan Buckhantz entered the ring once again. His $80 million lawsuit had been dropped. Instead he initiated an action against Gilliam, Schühly, Columbia Pictures and others claiming "unfair competition." A California superior court eventually ordered Columbia Pictures to include a disclaimer to the film indicating that the picture was a new work and without direct relation to the 1943 film. Around the time of the ruling, Buckhantz suffered a heart attack. It seemed even those outside the production team were not free from the malevolent hand of the Munchausen curse.

A Glimmering of Light

The cost of the production continued to escalate, and the burden to meet these expenses bounced back and forth between Film Finances and Lloyd's of London. Despite the misgivings of the financiers, one simple truth was evident to all involved: Millions had already been spent and the point of no return had long since passed. There was only one real solution that remained: to continue shooting and press forward at any cost, weathering the storm until the baron's adventures came to an end.

The fictional adventures of the baron put to the page by Raspe exhibited all of the despair and fortitude seen on Gilliam's set. In one section of the book, the destitute but ever-persevering protagonist remarks, "As soon as I perceived a glimmering of light I called out lustily to be released from a situation in which I was now almost suffocated." The production just barely bobbed on the surface, sometimes sinking below only to surface once again, gasping for air.

Even the conclusion to principal photography provided little relief from the demands of the picture. There still remained a musical score to compose and countless special effects shots to complete. One hundred forty-five miniature model shots remained on the production schedule, which were meant to help carry the narrative of the picture and the continuity of Gilliam's vision. Many of these sequences involved even greater complexity than the scenes shot at Cinecittà studios. A factor often overlooked when budgeting for the time and money commanded by these scenes was Gilliam's compulsion for perfection. Each scene had to flawlessly match even the most subtle nuances of the images locked in Gilliam's imagination. Yet, when the preliminary prints were complete, there was still one unanswered question that lingered. Would *The Adventures of Baron Munchausen* be a coherent, entertaining and commercially viable film?

The only way to gain a verdict in the court of public opinion was to screen the film for test audiences. Interviews and preview cards completed at the end of the screening often give a sense of the general public's reaction. In the case of *Munchausen*, the results of the postscreening focus groups revealed disastrous news; the audience hated it. Several people exited the theater before the film even ended. The paltry ratings from those who did stay from beginning to end made Columbia nervous about their prospects for a successful release. How does a studio pro-

mote a movie they know to be a disappointment? One major identified problem was the lack of familiarity American audiences had
with the source material. What seemed even more foreboding
than these initial test numbers was the film's performance in Germany, where the baron is a widely recognized and revered character. Munchausen failed to attract significant audiences even in
his homeland.

Columbia initially screened the film in just forty-six theaters
upon release in the United States. As the weeks passed, the number of screens grew to 88, then 92, then 106. The final total of
prints released came to 120, yielding a scant $8 million in ticket
sales. The final cost of the production, which reached $46.34 mil-
lion by the time it was completed, would have required a box
office gain of $200 million just to break even. Though the film's
poor ticket sales can be partially attributed to the unique nature
of a film that defies Hollywood norms, it was also the result of a
severely limited advertising and marketing campaign.

Gilliam recalled wryly, "Everything about Munchausen—the
movie—was a lie," referring, in part, to the rampant public rumors
about the production and spending. His final assessment of the
picture is bleak, yet not without hope, like the capricious forces of
fate affecting Munchausen himself. "There's no stopping certain
kinds of films once you set off and the train leaves the station, and
this was one of them. It's the one experience I find hardest to talk
about because it is so painful. It went out of control. I was the one
person who knew we couldn't finish the film, but it was my secret
that I had to carry every day, knowing there was no way the film
would ever be finished. I was like the black mulch, that filthy, dark
stuff that beautiful flowers grow out of."[27]

Despite the stress, arguments and frustrations that were such
consistent themes during production, Gilliam had, in the end,

completed a movie he had desperately wanted to make. Though the final cut was miles from the grand design he had envisioned so long ago when first opening the pages of Raspe's text, Gilliam had a film with moments he adored, however brief they might be. "For me, the film has got little stepping stones through it that I think are wonderful. The rest I'll tell you about in five years," he said.[28] It seemed to Gilliam in retrospect that the creation of the film demanded that he take the same journey of tiresome defeat, punctuated by fleeting victories, that the baron took himself. "It's always this way: the making of the film *is* the film," he concluded.[29]

Gilliam's next project was an audacious attempt to adapt Alan Moore's celebrated 1986 graphic novel *Watchmen* to the screen. He eventually abandoned the project. Even for an imagination as sprawling as Gilliam's, the scope of the picture could not fit within the limits of a feature-length film. "That was a really difficult one, because I thought it was such a wonderful book, and I didn't see how we could condense it and not destroy it at the same time. I was never totally comfortable with the project: I really thought it should have been a five-part miniseries for television, and then you would have had the time to develop the characters as they developed in the book."[30]

Gilliam's more recent works have also given way to the forces of man and nature, as he found himself struggling to support the collapsing project of *The Man Who Killed Don Quixote* in 2000. His effort to bring to life the 1605 story of the befuddled adventurer was as short-lived as the torrential downpours that literally washed away the set, while crippling health problems forced the lead actor, Jean Rochefort, to exit the production permanently. More disappointment awaited Gilliam when *The Brothers Grimm* made it to the silver screen in 2005, only to be met with a tepid reception by critics, who dismissed the picture as style over substance.

Many of the most trying times of his productions have been characterized by bitter feuds with studios and producers who never seem to be in agreement with Gilliam's tangled imagination and yearning for madness on the screen. In recent years, this has left him eager to absolve himself from the accountants and financiers of the typical studio system of filmmaking. Gilliam's desire to do things his way was apparent in his attempt to spread the word about his 2005 release *Tideland* on the street to a group of audience members waiting in line outside *The Daily Show with Jon Stewart*. He carried a slab of cardboard with rough lettering on the front reading, "Studio-less filmmaker, family to support, will direct for food."

This string of hardships has influenced Gilliam's reputation, causing many to believe that for reasons unknown he is simply prone to misfortune when orchestrating any kind of production. Others see the cause to these troubles as less fatalistic, citing Gilliam's insistence on perfection and the nature of his limitless creativity paired with a lack of organization. A headline in a September 8, 2004, issue of the satirical newspaper the *Onion* joked, "Terry Gilliam Barbecue Plagued by Production Delays."

The memory of making the film is an unpleasant one for many involved, especially Gilliam. Yet, beneath the lines on his face that are now distant reminders of the *Munchausen* struggle, there is still a childlike awe in Gilliam, a man who has seen enough conniving and swindling to corrupt anyone's innocence. For him, the experience is one of many in a life that always proves to be incredible, even if manifestly difficult at times. "Most people don't look at the world in a fantastical or magical way, but I still find the place pretty extraordinary," Gilliam said. "I like surprises, even when they're awful ones like this film! It makes life more interesting."[31] Perhaps Gilliam himself is more believable as a literary creation than as a living man. Like the misguided adventures of Don Quixote or the outrageous travels of the Baron Munchausen, Gilliam too has consigned his journeys and his pictures to the capricious forces of fate. Sometimes the outcome is a bang, at other times a whimper.

In recent years, his dissatisfaction with the Hollywood machine has extended to a pronounced disaffection with his home country. Though many of his films have been shot and produced in the United States, Gilliam decided to renounce his American citizenship in 2006. When asked why he made this choice he tersely remarked, "I thought I'd just simplify my life. I'm getting old. I'm going to die."[32] Yet, it has never seemed Gilliam's style to simplify. While Gilliam may be coming to terms with his mortality, he can certainly rest assured that the strife of days past will fade, while the flickering images of his work remain. Gilliam now smiles when remembering the disaster that was *Munchausen* and is even able to laugh at the executives who stood in opposition. "The good thing is they're all gone, and *Munchausen* is still around. Some of them are dead, some of them are probably in some old folks home, some are probably running studios, another form of death, and we're alive."[33]

Gilliam presses forward, still committed to his vision. And while his vision is unique, it seems most noble when viewed as part of a chain of storytelling that existed long before his time and will continue to exist long after. His art will unquestionably inspire more art, just as Gilliam was inspired by artists like Raspe and Doré. Even before *Munchausen,* there was Voltaire's Candide, a young man who experienced equally absurd and agonizing adventures. He begins his journey believing that all things exist with purpose and that even disastrous events, which have the most elusive causes, are in fact part of a grand metaphysical design. Like Gilliam, Candide also learned that some experiences offer no explanations, only new positions from which to grow. Early in life, Candide believes that "stones were made to be hewn and to construct castles." For Gilliam, there are still more castles to create and plenty of stones with which to build them.

4

"The Idiodyssey"
Apocalypse Now

There's a Place in France

ALONG THE COBBLED STREETS of Montmartre in northern Paris, the French playwright Oscar Méténier purchased an abandoned chapel at the end of the nineteenth century and converted it into a 293-seat theater. Each night, it was filled with a curious and awestruck audience gaping at the blood-soaked terror and dismemberment that washed across the stage. A single ticket to Le Théâtre du Grand Guignol allowed the viewer to enjoy several one-acts drawn from a repertoire of over a thousand sordid tales of murder, torture, lust and vengeance. The festering wounds and disfigured bodies on stage drew audiences from around the world with show titles like *Orgy in the Lighthouse* and *The Laboratory of Hallucinations*. Night after night body parts tumbled across the stage and eyes were scooped from the sockets of the actors, an effect made convincing with the use of real eyeballs purchased from a taxidermist to ensure a lifelike bounce as they hit the stage floor. Intestines strewn about were fresh acquisitions of the bovine variety from a nearby butcher shop. Drench them in blood, dim the lights, and they're convincing enough to induce fainting—a common, even nightly, occurrence in the theater.

Every night the actors were victims of the writers' distorted imaginations. One actress named Maxa held the dubious honor of being said to have died over 10,000 times in more than sixty sinister ways, including being guillotined, hanged, quartered, torched and shot. With so many simulations of death, one can imagine that more than one or two plays crossed briefly into reality. One actress nearly died when the stage apparatus used to create the illusion of a hanging malfunctioned. In another instance, a performer was seriously burned when the flame of a revolver came too close to his skin. However, many of the effects were achieved with the use of simple stage conventions—bladders filled with fake blood, anchovies made to look like crushed human tissue—all made realistic through grandiose performances and the willingness of the audience to believe.

The scripted material delved into a vibrant array of taboo subjects. Rape, infidelity, insanity and sodomy were all standard plots for the productions. For sixty-five years, audiences couldn't get enough, and the theater blasted out lurid tales one after another. But eventually something unexpected happened: People slowly stopped buying tickets. Audiences no longer felt shocked by gratuitous violence. Something more real and more horrifying began: World War II. The bloodshed on stage was a paltry facsimile compared to the all-too-real headlines and images of war. For those who watched loved ones swept off to battle, the Grand Guignol Theater was a meaningless excursion into a world of violence merely for the sake of violence. Isolated from the reality of the world, the theater became entranced by its own bloody legacy and madness. The theater's last director remarked, "Before the war, everyone felt that what was happening onstage was impossible. Now we know that these things, and worse, are possible in reality."[1]

In 1962, as the Vietnam War intensified, the Grand Guignol shut its doors forever. Terror and fear were the realities of daily life and could be seen on the nightly news with the flip of a switch. Violence was no longer confined to a shadowy road in the eighteenth arrondissement of Paris.

There were plenty of universal fears to be mined from the headlines of bloodshed in Vietnam. Yet, one of the most lasting fictional characters inspired by the war was a man evil enough to be a direct incarnation of the Grand Guignol. Colonel Kurtz was a central character in the film *Apocalypse Now*, which was inspired by Joseph Conrad's novel *Heart of Darkness*. The character brought to life by director Francis Ford Coppola was meant to be as brutal and malicious as the characters of the dark French theater, evoking images of victims' distended bodies strewn across the stage. Just as the evening shows strived for shocking violence, so too did Colonel Kurtz.

In time, it would become evident that this disturbing character, portrayed by Marlon Brando, would remain comfortably in the realm of mere fiction, but the struggle to tell the story would become a maddening nightmare.

"We Were Promised World War III"

"I always thought of Vietnam as a California war," said screenwriter John Milius.[2] Milius has the look of a general—an immovable, cantankerous, stalwart commander. He may well have been a marine if it weren't for his chronic asthma. "It was totally demoralizing," he admitted.[3]

The characters he created in his most famous work, *Apocalypse Now*, reflected his sentiment about a "California war." Many of the soldiers were young, free-spirited boys, looking to surf the next wave. Milius himself is a fan of surfing, but his membership on the board of the National Rifle Association and his early private school education in Colorado seem at odds with this distinctly West Coast sport. It is these unexpected contradictions that make Milius as interesting as any of his own characters. In fact, the Coen brothers did make him into a character; the volatile, unrelenting, gun-wielding Walter Sobchak in *The Big Lebowski* was based on Milius's unique personality and staunch conservative leanings.

During his childhood, he remembered, "We were promised World War III."[4] This remark betrays a sense of disappointment that so many of the flares and spent shell casings of his world remain only as images on the screen. Though, he insisted, "I've led my whole life behind enemy lines" as a vocal conservative in Hollywood.[5] "I've always been considered a nut. They kind of tolerate me. It's certainly affected me. I've been blacklisted for a large part of my career because of my politics—as surely as any writer was blacklisted back in the 1950s. It's just that my politics are from the other side, and Hollywood always veers left."[6]

Though his name may not be as well known as Francis Ford Coppola's, his lines certainly are: "I love the smell of napalm in the morning," spoken by Robert Duvall, as well as Dirty Harry's famous, "You've gotta ask yourself one question, 'Do I feel lucky?'" The poignant monologue in *Jaws* about the USS *Indianapolis* was his uncredited contribution. Aside from Coppola, Milius's tenure on *Apocalypse Now* is unrivaled. "I was ten years on that film. . . . I had the longest tour of duty," he said.[7] He wrote ten drafts of the screenplay, totaling over 1,000 pages, a clear indication of the interminable effort it took to capture the essence of the Vietnam War. It was an impressive feat for someone who has claimed to have grown up with "the worst possible work ethic, which is being a surfer."[8]

While attending the University of Southern California in 1962, a film professor told Milius's class, "Nobody could lick *Heart of Darkness.*"[9] Published in 1902, Joseph Conrad's classic novella tells the story of an Englishman named Marlow who travels the Congo River on a ferryboat to trade ivory and retrieve Kurtz, a rogue ivory collector entrenched in the jungle. The challenge of bringing the story to the screen was too tempting for Milius to ignore. "That was like waving a red flag in front of a young bull, you know. That was the worst thing he could say. I immediately set out to make *Heart of Darkness.*"[10]

He had read Conrad's work many years earlier, when he was seventeen, and he insisted that he would not go back and reread it because he didn't want to spoil his initial impressions and his subsequent memories of the story. The original title of Milius's screenplay was *The Psychedelic Soldier*, which would later be changed after Milius became inspired by a popular pin which read "Nirvana Now," a motto of hippie culture.

In 1969 Coppola agreed to give Milius $25,000 to write the screenplay, including an opportunity to earn an additional 12.5 percent of the film's net profits. As source material, Milius would also draw upon the work of journalist Michael Herr, who wrote extensively on the Vietnam War for *Esquire* magazine between 1967 and 1968. Herr's firsthand experience gave him direct insight into the chaos and filth of this "rock 'n' roll war." One article in particular, "The Battle for Khe Sanh," was a major inspiration for the tone of Milius's screenplay. In 1977 his articles were compiled as a collection titled *Dispatches*, largely considered the definitive distillation of the war. The style of dialogue in *Apocalypse Now* invites numerous comparisons to Herr's work. Additionally, Herr's contribution to the picture is most seen in the memorable voice-over dialogue, which Herr himself wrote. The language and voice of this component of the film were largely derived from his one-year stay in Vietnam, where he witnessed the fighting without deadlines or any specific assignments that otherwise would have likely left him tied down to certain locations. In one section of *Dispatches* titled "Breathing In," Herr describes a marine turning to him in the middle of a battle and saying, "Okay, man, you go on, you go on out of here, you cocksucker, but I mean it, you tell it! You tell it, man."[11] Herr would go on to help cowrite *Full Metal Jacket* with Gustav Hasford and Stanley Kubrick.

The revision process for Milius's script began in 1975 as initial budgets were planned. Preliminary calculations indicated that the cost of the picture would fall between $12 million and $14 million. The film would be made under Coppola's own company, Zoetrope, which he formed in the late 1960s with filmmaker George Lucas and producer Mona Skager. Projections showed that preparations for the film would consume three to four months, with an anticipated shooting start date of January 1976. The completion of principal photography was not expected to last longer than six months. They decided to shoot in the Philippines, a decision that was reached after the U.S. Army's Chief Information Office at the Pentagon refused to provide any kind of assistance to the production. The distant location proved to be a challenge when it came time to cast the main character, Willard. The rigorous production required an actor with substantial talent and unflappable stamina in order to endure the limited amenities and stifling jungle heat. Steve McQueen seemed an easy choice, but his requested fee of $3 million was too great to accept, especially in light of initial disagreements between Coppola and the actor regarding the script.

This delay in casting prompted the first of many financial difficulties. Coppola's original distribution guarantees had been formed on the very basis of McQueen starring in this central role. Without his commitment to the film, much of this funding was lost, forcing Coppola to support the film with his own capital. It was an early setback that only added to the struggle of a hard-won financing agreement with United Artists when negotiations with Warner Bros. and Columbia failed. Other potential leading men fell like dominos. James Caan, Al Pacino and Robert Redford all turned down the role for a variety of reasons. Tommy Lee Jones and Nick Nolte were also considered. Many of the actors who turned down the role felt that the prospect of a shoot in the Philippines was too taxing, even though shooting time was originally scheduled to last no longer than four months. Eventually Harvey Keitel came on board to play Willard, but as a result of so many leading men turning the role down, it was reported that "Coppola felt abandoned by people whose careers he felt he had significantly advanced."[12]

Coppola had already spent a million dollars from his own pocket on the preproduction process, and he was ready to make the film a reality. An exhaustive list of props was prepared, cataloging an eclectic range of items, such as fishing boats, Zippo lighters and artificial marijuana plants to be used for the sprawling set of Kurtz's temple at the end of the picture. In the meantime, 350 locals were recruited to construct another enormous set piece, a 700-foot bridge made of coconut logs. Among the most important props, of course, were the Huey helicopters, on loan from the Philippine Air Force. The entire country's stock consisted of only twenty-four functional helicopters, fifteen of which Coppola planned to use in a dawn attack scene. However, maintaining control of this resource would prove difficult. President Ferdinand Marcos often led surprise attacks against "communist" rebels that inhabited a small group of southern islands, which forced Coppola to relinquish the helicopters without warning. Each day, the helicopters had to be painted with authentic U.S. Army markings in the morning and repainted with their Philippine Air Force decals in the evening. There was little doubt among the cast and crew that they had all ventured a long way from the sunny hills of Hollywood.

"The Idiodyssey"

By March 20, 1976, Coppola was with his family in Manila and ready to shoot the first scene. Things started poorly when Keitel and a few others on a raft got stuck on a river, an incident that presented an unsettling resemblance to the story. This uncomfortable start to filming preceded much more serious problems as it became increasingly clear to Coppola that he would have to make an enormous change to the film. He had envisioned the character of Willard as a man who was an observer, somewhat passive in nature like Conrad's Marlow. Keitel's acting style imbued the role with a certain fierceness and intensity, which made Willard a more active character than he was intended to be on paper. Keitel had been miscast, and something had to be done. Coppola resolved to fire him. The unpleasantness of the decision was somewhat tempered by Keitel's acknowledgment that the part was really not for him. Remarkably, Coppola was able to find a replacement in only a week—Martin Sheen. He was one of the many actors originally approached to star in the film, but prior obligations had kept him from accepting the role. His schedule had since cleared up, and he was now free to join the cast. Though casting this central role was a milestone for the project after so many failed attempts, it did not come without the portent of more substantial problems. Coppola struggled with limited physical resources as a result of his unsuccessful negotiations with the U.S. Department of Defense. Despite the agreement with President Marcos, the production was in desperate need of additional helicopters and equipment. Perhaps equally as important was Coppola's need for strong technical advisers to assist in the logistics of the complex battle sequences. In late April, Coppola reached out to Secretary of Defense Donald Rumsfeld. He shared the script with him and made his request for the privilege to rent U.S. aircrafts. It was likely a humbling effort on the part of the director who had already encountered frustrating resistance from the government. But the unreliability and disorganization of his partnership with the Philippine Air Force had exhausted his patience.

The military was hesitant to cooperate, citing certain elements of the script as the greatest point of contention. They agreed to permit rentals to *Apocalypse Now* only if the story was significantly altered. Instead of a seek-and-destroy mission, they wanted Willard to be following a directive to apprehend and return any soldiers guilty of war crimes so that they could be properly tried or referred for psychiatric treatment. Coppola was willing to offer a slightly revised version of the script, which put less responsibility for the mission on the U.S. military, but this change was not enough for the Department of Defense. They rejected the request, leaving Coppola without any additional aircraft. He had no choice but to press forward with the old equipment.

Coordinating the team of helicopters was especially important for the napalm attack scene, one of the picture's signature shots. The crew dug a deep trench next to a long tree line, and the corridor was filled with 1,200 gallons of gasoline that would all be ignited in just ninety seconds. A group of F-5 jets would fly overhead, dropping artificial napalm canisters as the gasoline ignited, in order to complete the illusion of an aerial attack. The special effects crew had just one chance to get it right. The camera was positioned a half mile away. An immense wave of heat caused by the eruption wafted over the crew, but they got their shot. It would be a rare moment of precision after painstaking preparations.

The unique logistical problems in filming a narrative as sprawling as *Apocalypse Now* were endless. Each stunt or explosion was of such scale and originality that the approach to executing it had to be just as original. One brief scene called for a tiger to leap out of a thicket toward two actors. The animal had to be flown in from Los Angeles, which required a transfer to another plane to get to the Philippines. The second leg of the trip was particularly challenging, as Eleanor Coppola, Francis's wife, remembered, "The passengers were in their seats when they put the tiger's carrying box on the plane. They placed a chicken by the door of the box, but when they walked the tiger on, instead of taking the chicken and going into it, he jumped on top of the box and was staring down at the passengers. . . . The pilot climbed out his window onto the wing and just sat there, refusing to fly."[13]

As if the logistical problems of the set weren't enough, one of the most difficult challenges of the production was the weather. Typhoon Olga gathered strength as production started, and heavy rains began to hinder shooting. Coppola continued to shoot many of the scenes despite the inclement weather. In just six days, the cast and crew weathered forty inches of rain. Coppola recalled the nearly laughable circumstances that led to such crushing bad luck for the sets. "A storm came in off the South China Sea, split, and one part hit one obscure town, the other part hit another obscure town two hundred miles away—and both were our main sets. How can you take it seriously?"[14]

After the storm, the production was shut down for six weeks while Coppola and the team tried to regain their footing. They had ninety hours of exposed film and had already spent $7 million, which was $3 million over budget. "Francis felt hopeless and scared,"[15] Eleanor recalled. United Artists had to shoulder this cost, but ultimately Coppola had to pay it all back if the film failed to earn $40 million or more.

The problems were not limited to finances and bad weather. More abstract issues began to emerge for Coppola as he spent the shooting break reviewing the structure of the script. The more discussion the team had about the themes and characters, the more incoherent the narrative became, until the message of the story seemed as fleeting and ineffable as the haze lifting from the jungle. One journalist reported, "In frustrating moments, Coppola dubbed the film 'the idiodyssey.'"[16]

Despite the numerous struggles that came with refining the story, the central problem was simple: The script was not finished. This only complicated Coppola's negotiations with Marlon Brando regarding how best to portray the character of Colonel Kurtz. The actor was resistant to the idea that a decorated and accomplished leader like Kurtz would turn into a drug-addicted hippie.

In stark contrast, Martin Sheen was all too willing to embrace the deeply embattled essence of his character, Willard. Just one day after shooting recommenced, the lead actor hit rock bottom. It was Sheen's thirty-sixth birthday, and Coppola happened to be shooting a scene in which Willard experiences a mental breakdown in a hotel room. Sheen became drunk, just as his character is described in the script, and completely unhinged. He began to mimic judo fight stances in front of the mirror. In his drunken stupor, he accidentally struck the mirror and it shattered onto the floor. His hand began to bleed profusely as Willard, and Sheen himself, grappled with his disturbed state of mind. The crew considered stopping the scene, but Sheen convinced them to continue, saying, "I'm not hurt, I want to explore this."[17]

Decades later, Sheen still vividly recalled the scene. "At the time, I was a drinker. Hell, I was an alcoholic. It was my thirty-sixth birthday and I'd been drinking all day. He's in a hotel room, waiting for a job. He's on his third tour, a lonely alcoholic, just been divorced—that's what all those papers are about that he's rolling around in. And also, in a sense, he's become his enemy—eating in a crouched position, adapted to the environment. Those were the elements. I was swacked—couldn't hardly stand up. Francis tried to stop me when I hit the mirror—myself, the enemy—and I said, 'No, stay away. I want this for me.' I felt I wanted to wrestle this demon. It was planned, but unplanned. When the rushes came in, I said, 'No, I never want to see that.' And I never did, until it was released."[18] Assistant director Jerry Ziesmer, who also spoke the famous line "Terminate with extreme prejudice" in the film, explained, "Francis wanted to see Willard come out of Martin Sheen, for Marty to reveal the assassin inside Willard."[19] Understandably, Ziesmer had concerns about the moral implications of the decision to continue filming and wondered, "Should we have pushed and prodded Marty to the extent we did for a performance in a motion picture? Did the end justify the means?"[20] The nervous breakdown was only one of several physical and psychological sufferings Sheen faced during the production.

Scenes Unknown

The evolving script presented less and less of a resemblance to Milius's original work. The dialogue changed every day, which placed great demands on the actors to continue memorizing lines even as the shoot progressed. Sometimes Coppola would write a new draft for a scene on a four-by-six-inch index card. The scenes on the call sheet for the day were sometimes as ephemeral as catching the ripples behind the patrol boat as it traveled upriver toward some obscure character. Some pages simply read "Scenes Unknown."

This indecisiveness, or artistic capriciousness, of the production resulted in a steady flow of budget overages. Despite the uncontrollable factor of weather, much of the additional spending was the result of a collective perception that the demands of the picture were being met by some inexhaustible financial resource. In fact, there was a limit to how far United Artists could extend their bottom line. But for a well-known director of such great achievements, it seemed no request was too excessive, even though nearly all materials and equipment had to be flown in from the United States at tremendous expense. "All of us were at fault. First of all, there were too many of us in the Philippines making the movie. All of us worked to please Francis Ford Coppola, the world's most respected director. If he asked for a hundred explosives, we prepared five hundred. . . . To please him we felt we could never tell him 'No,' and in order not to do that we all bought more, hired more, rented more," Ziesmer said.[21] In pursuit of authenticity, some went above and beyond the call of duty. Eleanor Coppola recalled visiting the temple set: "I heard there are some real cadavers in body bags at the Kurtz Compound set. I asked the propman about it. He said, 'The script says a pile of burning bodies, it doesn't say a pile of burning dummies.'"[22]

Milius's ambitious and complex French plantation scene exemplified such attention to detail and inattention to spending. Set decorator George Nelson rifled through private art collections and rented expensive antique furniture for the colonial house, all of which had to be flown in. In response to critics who accused him of frivolous spending, Coppola quipped, "I don't see why this amount shouldn't be spent on a morality story, when you can spend it on a giant gorilla, a little fairy tale like *The Wiz* or some jerk who flies up in the sky."[23] Despite his defensive attitude, Coppola, perhaps more than anyone else, was most aware of the escalating costs. With each dollar spent, he became more indebted to the picture, or what he hoped would one day become a picture. In addition to equipment, pyrotechnics and helicopters, time itself was an expensive commodity. The French plantation scene had to be shot during the magic hour, a brief period at dusk when the sun, nearing the horizon, casts a distinct golden light. Originally slated for two days, the shooting of a scene at a dining room table consumed five days of production. One actress in the scene, Aurore Clément, remarked, "Every detail in the scene was right, right for the meaning." She continued, "Francis wanted to have absolutely perfect white and red—Chateau Latour—wine on the table."[24] Journalist Peter Cowie reported, "The bottle of 1954 Latour wine was an empty one, transported carefully from Coppola's own mantelpiece in San Francisco."[25] Coppola dictated the following guidelines for the scene at the dining room table: "White wine should be served ice cold, red wine should be served at about fifty-eight degrees, it should be opened approximately an hour to an hour and a half, even two hours before served. I want the French to say, 'My God, how did they do that?'"[26]

The lost time only added pressure to the multitude of scenes that lay ahead, which taxed the patience of the cast and crew. When Marlon Brando was cast in the film, his weight came in at well over 200 pounds, clearly at odds with the description of Kurtz as a withered, malarial madman in the script. In Joseph Conrad's novella, Kurtz "looked seven feet long. His covering had fallen off, and his body emerged from it pitiful and appalling as from a winding-sheet. I could see the cage of his ribs all astir, the bones of his arm waving."[27] Brando fasted to rapidly shed pounds, but his five-week commitment to the film left little time to adjust his ample weight, or the costumes that had been prepared for a slimmer Brando. "Marlon is very overweight. Francis and he are struggling with how to change the character in the script. Brando wants to camouflage his weight and Francis wants to play him as a man eating all the time and overindulging," wrote Eleanor Coppola.[28]

It was ultimately decided that he would be shot veiled in shadows, wearing black to conceal his weight. Many shots were filmed from the neck up, focusing more of the action on his monologue rather than his frame. The bulk of the original dialogue was jettisoned as Coppola and Brando utilized improvisation, cue cards and commands transmitted through an earpiece to complete the scenes. Ultimately, these long-form shots were cut down to more manageable lengths. Reinventing the character in this way was likely their only choice, given that Brando had not read *Heart of Darkness* as he was asked to. Production assistant Doug Claybourne remarked, "Francis had to literally start from scratch with him. He had to bring him up to speed on what the thing was about and who the character was."[29] These preparations consumed further valuable time as hundreds of cast and crew members could not move forward with filming until Coppola and Brando agreed on how best to portray Kurtz.

The intensity of the production reached a breaking point in early March when Martin Sheen suffered a heart attack. "I went blind for a few moments, my extremities froze, I couldn't control my feet and I began hallucinating. I was crawling by the end, but I kept talking to myself all the way. I knew that if I went unconscious that would be it. The strange thing was that it wasn't frightening, or even that painful—I've had worse pain in a dentist chair. I knew that I could have called it quits if I wanted to, and in fact there was something in my head that kept saying, 'O.K., let it go.'"[30]

In an attempt to suppress rumors, the production cited heat exhaustion as the reason for Sheen's hospitalization. His condition was so severe that a priest was brought in to deliver the last rites. In the end, he suffered no serious damage to his heart, but he would be unable to begin filming again for several weeks. During his recovery, the crew tackled many shots that did not require Sheen. They even got some distant shots of Willard by using Sheen's brother Joseph as a stand-in. For any other film, an event like this would likely have shut down production temporarily, but the project was too far advanced to stop it completely. It was not immediately clear that Sheen would be able to return to the set at all, but there was a collective belief that a man in his early thirties would have the resilience to recover quickly. And, in fact, Sheen was back in front of the camera on April 19. It had been just over one year since the shooting had begun.

The cast and crew pressed forward, anxious to complete the shoot and return home to family, friends, new projects and new chapters of their lives. The punishing heat left many people weak and frail, some shedding twenty pounds or more over the course of the shoot. They managed their stress with good doses of heavy drinking and partying. Production assistant Claybourne remembered, "At the hotel where the crew was based, it was party heaven. We'd have a hundred beers lined up around the swimming pool. There were people diving off the roofs, it was crazy."[31] But after fourteen months, the project was not even near completion; 1.5 million feet of exposed film remained coiled up in spools, waiting to be viewed, cut and arranged. They had 250 hours of footage, representing several disparate narratives all with different meanings, different outcomes and different messages. Coppola reflected, "The way we made it was very much like the Americans were in Vietnam. We were in the jungle, there were too many of us, we had access to too much money, too much equipment, and little by little we went insane."[32]

The Gordian Knot

Ultimately, it was decided that a voice-over narration would be needed to turn the obscure narrative of the picture into a cohesive whole. Many scenes had numerous possible interpretations with different inflections, lines, looks and nuances. Michael Herr, who wrote the narration, would help guide the decision process with his insight into Willard's thoughts. Over thirty-five sessions were required to complete the tracks, and the arrangement of the pieces still remained.

Coppola's challenge of unearthing a film from a tangle of footage was not unlike the legend of the Gordian knot. In 333 BCE, Alexander the Great and his army arrived in Gordium on their way across Anatolia. In Gordium there was a wagon tied to a post within the Temple of Zeus. The prophecy of the time told that anyone able to unravel the massive knot that secured the wagon would one day become the ruler of Asia. Alexander went to the temple and examined the endless coils of the knot. Then he drew his sword and simply cut the knot in half.

Confronting the result of so many months of shooting did little to allay the ever-quaking fears that no one would be able to unravel the picture from the menacing tangles of Coppola's Gordian knot. As Coppola's journey continued, so did Willard's. Though the filming was complete, the ending to the story was still unknown, given the numerous outcomes that could be configured from the raw footage. Eleanor cogently observed, "The film Francis is making is a metaphor for a journey into self. He has made that journey and is still making it. It's scary to watch someone you love go into the center of himself and confront his fears, fear of failure, fear of death, fear of going insane. You have to fail a little, die a little, go insane a little to come out the other side. The process is not over for Francis."[33]

Coppola considered a variety of endings. One version consisted of an air strike on the Kurtz compound, which erupts in fire and smoke in a sort of deus ex machina that utterly annihilates everyone and everything around it. In another version Willard completes his mission, killing Kurtz and emerging from his temple with a machete in hand only to find Kurtz's followers standing at attention to him, their new leader. An abrupt fade-out leaves the viewer to wonder if Willard will stay or return home. Neither of these two versions was well received by audiences or critics.

The threat of being left without any discernable story only added to the pressure already experienced during the shoot. "Francis told me one day, 'I've got to do this picture,'" John Milius remembered. "'I consider it the most important picture I will ever make. If I die making it, you'll take over, if you die, George Lucas will take over.'"[34] It was Coppola's responsibility to bring the film to completion and realize the contributions and hard-won achievements of actors. Robert Duvall recalled, "I was so sick and frustrated with the picture that when I did the scene, I did something which wasn't in the script. I threw a prop twenty feet in the air. Coppola screamed, 'Cut! That was terrific!' He came over to me and said, 'How did you have such an inspiration?' I said, 'I did it because I couldn't take your goddamn tantrums any longer!'"[35]

The press became increasingly skeptical that *Apocalypse Now* would be a decent movie, let alone an intelligent one with a coherent message. The enormity of the costs made journalists anxious to dismiss the work in progress as a blunder, no matter what the outcome. One reporter summarized, "Hollywood today is much like an East Texas oilfield with wildcatters willing to sink a dozen dry holes to achieve one fabled gusher. At the moment, Francis Ford Coppola is the most spectacular speculator, sinking most of his own capital into the $25-million Vietnam War epic."[36] It was likely clear to everyone outside and within the production that Coppola had taken an incredible financial risk and that a portion of this money was spent irresponsibly as a result of miscommunication and miscalculation. However, there is little indication that Coppola had any goal outside of making the most artistic film he possibly could.

The uncertainty surrounding the completion of the film came to exact a physical toll on Coppola as well. One day on set, he simply collapsed. Stress, paralyzing depression and exhaustion were likely the main contributing factors. Executives at United Artists were probably not far from suffering similar bouts of spontaneous breakdown, given their $25 million investment in a film that had yet to be edited. Postproduction would eventually cost $10 million, a sum Coppola had to provide all on his own, which he acquired in part by mortgaging his Pacific Heights home in San Francisco. While many were freed from the picture after the last day of shooting on May 21, 1977, Francis would retreat to the confines of the recording studio and editing room. Some journalists began calling the movie *Apocalypse When*.

Biographer Gene D. Phillips wrote, "During post-production, in the fall of 1977, Coppola was diagnosed by a psychiatrist as having manic-depressive tendencies, for which lithium, a tranquilizer, was prescribed. Because Coppola did not want it bandied about Hollywood that he was taking medication, he arranged to have the prescription written under the name of Kurtz."[37] The mental strain was perhaps caused, in part, by the rapid shift from endless days of moving and shooting, to sitting and watching as the collaborative process of editing took shape. Initial editing culminated in a preliminary cut with an epic running time of seven hours. The following cut, made approximately six months later, included the voice-over narration written by Michael Herr and clocked in at five hours. Major portions still had to be removed to produce anything close to a marketable film.

The original ending, in which the Kurtz compound was destroyed in an ear-splitting aerial assault, failed to capture audiences during test screenings. The problem of the ending still persisted when the three-hour feature was first revealed on a large scale at the Cannes Film Festival in 1979. Coppola openly recognized the issues that still required resolution, calling the film "a work in progress." Regardless, the judges and audience loved the film, and it won the coveted Palme d'Or. The tremendous honor brought much-needed rejuvenation to those who had worked so tirelessly on the picture, but many of the film's first audience members still openly criticized the ambiguity of the ending.

By the time the film finally reached its premiere at the Ziegfeld Theatre in New York City on August 15, 1979, Coppola had settled on an ending that brought a greater sense of closure to the picture. The film garnered $311,000 during the first week in this particular theater, a good sign that the budget could move from red to black ink.

Though Coppola and his team had suffered plenty of bad press during the making of the film, it had the benefit of garnering attention, thus enticing people to see the picture when it went into wide release. Even President Jimmy Carter saw the movie during a private White House screening. Many felt the picture

116

was unsuccessful in its attempt to deliver a meaningful message about the Vietnam War. However, many others, including Roger Ebert, appreciated the stylistic and technical mastery that allowed the viewer to access the moods, emotions and images of the conflict. Ebert wrote, "I am not particularly interested in the 'ideas' in Coppola's film. Critics of *Apocalypse* have said that Coppola was foolish to translate *Heart of Darkness*, that Conrad's vision had nothing to do with Vietnam, and that Coppola was simply borrowing Conrad's cultural respectability to give a gloss to his own disorganized ideas. The same objection was made to the hiring of Brando: Coppola was hoping, according to this version, that the presence of Brando as an icon would distract us from the emptiness of what he's given to say." But, in reality, the film succeeds because it "achieves greatness not by analyzing our 'experience in Vietnam,' but by re-creating, in characters and images, something of that experience."[38]

In a review for *Variety*, Dale Pollock wrote, "*Apocalypse Now* was worth the wait. Alternately a brilliant and bizarre film, Francis Coppola's four year 'work in progress' offers the definitive validation to the old saw, 'War is hell.'" However, he later predicts that the film "will also have trouble avoiding political pigeonholing, since it's the first film to directly excoriate U.S. involvement in the Indochina war."[39] The *New Republic*, *Chicago Tribune* and *Washington Post* all responded with deflating criticism. They were especially disparaging of the anticlimactic revealing of Kurtz.

Despite these criticisms, the picture had earned approximately $82 million by the third quarter of 1982. The total cost of production was $30.5 million. The film earned eight Academy Award nominations and won the awards for Best Cinematography and Best Sound.

Since *Apocalypse Now*, Coppola has moved on to films of a

more manageable scale. So far, he has not attempted the challenges of a film as audacious, ambitious and complex as this signature work. The picture itself developed a life of its own, as numerous versions and different edits were produced, most notably *Apocalypse Now Redux*, released in 2001, which included previously deleted scenes.

It is unlikely that Coppola or any person associated with *Apocalypse Now* will ever again embark on a project so layered or taxing. The final cut was no more a realization of original intentions than the numerous re-edits were faithful to the original release. The Vietnam War took on different meanings and continues to do so as the perceptions of *Apocalypse Now* change against the morphing background of subsequent war films, many of which are in various ways influenced by Coppola's achievement. Decades later, Coppola has tempered his assessment of his turmoil in the sweltering jungle, saying, "With the perspective of years, let me say that notions of madness and nervous breakdowns during this time are exaggerated and were really much more your basic old-fashioned midlife crises."[40]

5

Adventure Is Over

Fitzcarraldo

Kingdom of Rust

I N 1967 A WORLD WAR II veteran named Roy Bates discovered a forgotten outpost in the international waters seven miles off the eastern shores of Britain. The island consisted of a platform 120 feet long and 50 feet wide, and it rested on two large concrete pillars rising 60 feet above the surface of the North Sea waters. It was just one of four naval sea forts used during World War II. Soldiers stationed on the structure watched for German enemies through the crosshairs of antiaircraft auto cannons and inhabited the interior seven floors of the concrete pillars, which were stocked with ammunition and food.

When the war ended, the guns were dismantled and shipped away. Though international law mandated that the nations that built the structures were obliged to remove them as well, they were simply abandoned, forgotten and left to rust. Years later, Roy Bates decided he would use the vacant location to broadcast his own pirate radio station. British territory extended just three miles out from the country's shore, so the platform was uniquely positioned to allow Bates distance from the law but a close proximity to his listening audience. Shortly after Bates and his son set up their broadcast equipment, Britain legalized pirated radio. It was then that Bates officially made the island his own, declaring it a sovereign principality under his personal rule. This was well within his rights; the platform was without ownership as a result of "dereliction of sovereignty."

Bates, now Prince Roy, his wife Princess Joan and their son Michael became the rulers of their own micro nation. Eventually they would have a flag, passports, currency, even stamps, all specially designed for what they called Sealand. It was their domain, and they would protect it. Their resolve was tested the following year, when they spotted a British vessel approaching their new home. Michael Bates fired a warning shot in an attempt to deter the possible enemies. Roy and Michael were subsequently brought to trial for this act. The judge rule, that, since it rested in international waters, their home was not subject to British jurisdiction. It was their castle, and they could defend it however they saw fit. They were exonerated.

But they were beset again in 1978, when a helicopter tried to land on the platform. Michael wouldn't let them touch down; his parents were on a business trip to Austria and he was alone on Sealand. Instead, a man descended from the helicopter on a winch wire. He told Michael that he was a German tax consultant and produced a telex from Roy indicating that Sealand had been sold and that Michael was to immediately hand it over to the men. Michael recalled, "To cut a long story short, I went into our living room—which at the time had just small portholes, no big double-glass windows—and the door got slammed, and there I was locked in this steel room. The windows were too small to get out of. There was literally no way out of the steel box."[1]

The business trip that Prince Roy and Princess Joan were taking was nothing more than a part of an elaborate scheme enacted by these men to pull Michael's parents away and claim Sealand for themselves. After three days in the locked steel room, Michael was dropped on a fishing trawler headed for the Netherlands. When his parents finally discovered the plot, they assembled a security team and called a friend who was a helicopter pilot. They rescued Michael, and then made a plan to reclaim their land at dawn.

With their friend hovering above the platform, Michael and his father—armed with a gun—repelled from the helicopter. The men immediately surrendered. From that day forward, Sealand was the family's irrevocable possession, a tiny principality surrounded by water, held up by concrete and one man's pursuit of a dream so unique and absurd that it defied all notions of the complicated world they abandoned. Today the United Kingdom does not recognize Sealand as a sovereign nation, though Prince Roy likes to remind people, "There are a lot of places that don't recognize Monaco."[2]

For some it seems that to conquer a dream is to conquer the world, and for one director named Werner Herzog, those two endeavors were so closely related that they may as well have been the same thing. His dream was to tell the true story of a man who also turned away from society in order to build an opera house in the unforgiving jungle of South America, hundreds of miles upstream from any semblance of civilization. In order to bring the building materials for his opera house, the character has to bring a steamboat deep into the jungle. But, in order to put the boat into the water, he must first hoist it over a steep tract of land. Herzog's struggle was to replicate this feat in its entirety, with no optical effects and no models.

"Adventure Is Over"

Who is Werner Herzog? The simplest answer is that he is a man who has devoted his life to the exploration of the fantastic through documentary filmmaking. His work posits a far more complicated inquiry: What compels him? This is a question that requires an exploration as circuitous and complex as any one of his films.

One could try to draw conclusions about his motivation by watching his films, as if each production is a facet of his character, like fractured light through a prism. But in matters of art and life, the whole is much greater than the sum of its parts. There is more to this director than his pictures; there is the process by which he makes them. He is a man who has embarked on unfathomable journeys to explore the essence of unfathomable subjects. This is true especially of his brutal experience in the sweltering jungles of Brazil and Peru, where the distinction between fiction and reality became blurred as he began channeling the same obsession as the central character of his film *Fitzcarraldo*.

Yet, Herzog will tell you, "I'm not an adventurer."[3] He says, "Adventure is over. Now you can book an adventure trip to New Guinea to see the headhunters. It has degenerated that far. Adventure belongs to a century when men would face each other in a pistol duel at dawn."[4] Ironically, his description of adventure sounds similar to an incident on the set of *Fitzcarraldo*, when he threatened to shoot his recalcitrant lead actor as he tried to renege on his contract. Herzog's career doesn't appear to have started with a fascination with films but rather with all things bizarre—an intense curiosity about those quiet, peculiar things that few people recognize but exist all around.

He grew up in a distant mountain village in Bavaria. His filmmaking began when he stole a 35 mm camera from a film school in the early 1960s. "I know it was not theft. I had a natural right to take it," he asserted.[5] He did not see his first film until well into his adolescence. "I did not even know the cinema existed until I was eleven, when a traveling projectionist arrived at the school house." He was seventeen when he made his first phone call. "I grew up without knowing technology," he explained.[6] Yet, the dilapidated conditions of his surroundings were fertile grounds from which his imagination would grow. "People always think that growing up in the ruins was such a bad thing for children. On the contrary, it was wonderful. We were the kings of bombed-out blocks in the cities. In the countryside, we were in possession of well-functioning firearms."[7]

Many of his films have brought him to landscapes even more striking than the war-ravaged grounds of his childhood. He has traveled to the Sahara desert to capture mirages on film. He filmed on the island of Guadeloupe after a volcanic eruption spurred a mass evacuation. Following the first Gulf War, he explored the barren, scorched terrain of Kuwait. More recently he traveled to Antarctica as part of a two-man production team. Herzog's ventures have given him something of a reputation for being a rogue director, though some of his more dangerous challenges were executed with great care. "I prefer to be alive," he stated matter-of-factly, "so I'm cautious about taking risks. And contrary to what rumors say and what the media reports about me, I'm a very circumspect and prudent person, and I eliminate danger as far as it can be done. And as proof, I can say that in fifty-eight films now, not one of my actors got injured, not one. So there must be something organized and prudent in me; I'm not just going blindly out for things like that."[8] Herzog once abandoned a project slated to shoot in Sudan during a bloody civil war. The fiercely inhospitable Himalayan mountain K2 was also to be a location for one of his features. Continuous avalanches made the logistics impossible and too dangerous for even Herzog. These projects were canceled only after long deliberation in the face of near suicidal ventures, though some were too enticing for Herzog to forgo. "Now I have to admit, I do not have a perfectly clean record," he revealed. "I did climb La Soufrière when it was in danger of erupting."[9]

Such foreboding landscapes are appropriate locations for Herzog—a man who fits well among the effulgent light of his subjects, often pulled into odd circumstances as frequently as he seeks them out. Listening to Herzog describe his process only invites more questions about his art, which unexpectedly conceals itself upon closer examination. "I never have searched for a subject. They always just come along. They never come by way of decision-making. They just haunt me. I can't get rid of them. I did not invite them."[10] He insists he is no thrill seeker, but he seems to carry a mystifying charge which constantly finds him intersecting with the uncanny. "My character has nothing to do with it—it's just statistics, abnormal statistics, even though nobody will believe me."[11]

There is no truer example of these uninvited subjects than a man named Klaus Kinski, the lead actor in *Fitzcarraldo* and a person whom no discussion of Herzog would be complete without exploring. Herzog recalled, "We had moved to Munich, and we lived in some sort of a boarding house, the four of us, my mother and my two brothers, so it was four persons in one room. One day, the owner of the place, an elderly lady who had a heart for starving artists, picked up Kinski literally from the street."[12] Herzog's magnetism for the uncanny had drawn this impossible character from nowhere and into his life. Kinski, an aspiring actor, had been squatting in an attic before being brought into Herzog's family, but the generosity of the woman who pulled him from these circumstances went entirely unrecognized. Like attempting to tame a wolf as a house pet, it immediately became clear that Kinski was a volatile force. Herzog recalled that Kinski frequently walked around naked, often shouting furiously and indecipherably. "From the very first moment I was terrorized," Herzog recalled. Kinski once locked himself in the bathroom for forty-eight hours straight and destroyed everything around him in a prolonged fit of rage. When he finally calmed down, all that was left of the bathroom was minuscule pieces of fixtures and furniture. "You could sift it through a tennis racket."[13] Kinski starred in one of Herzog's earliest films, *Aguirre: The Wrath of God*, a stunning narrative of a mad Spanish soldier leading a group of conquistadors on a journey to find the lost golden city of El Dorado. Made for only $370,000, the spectacle of landscapes and Kinski's mad demeanor certainly appear to have cost millions, and perhaps the sanity of those involved. The low budget of the production seems impossibly small when one considers that Kinski's salary amounted to one-third of the total, a sum the actor would no doubt argue was well worth it. During production, Herzog recalled Kinski saying, "The only fascinating landscape on this earth is the human face."[14]

The unhinged Kinski seemed to have an insufferable temper that could barely be contained by his own skin. Herzog once said that every gray hair on his head is named Kinski. The actor offered his response in kind. In his autobiography, *All I Need Is Love*, Kinski claimed that Herzog "doesn't care about anyone or anything except his wretched career as a so-called film-maker. Driven by a pathological addiction to sensationalism, he creates the most senseless difficulties and dangers, risking other people's safety and even their lives—just so he can eventually say that he, Herzog, has beaten seemingly unbeatable odds."[15] This is an unexpected denouncement from an actor who worked so tirelessly with Herzog on so many difficult films, the most difficult of which may have been *Fitzcarraldo*. However, as Herzog's films so consistently reveal, there is more below the surface. Kinski also wrote, "Herzog is a miserable, hateful, malevolent, avaricious, money-hungry, nasty, sadistic, treacherous, cowardly creep."[16] Yet, Herzog eventually revealed that he helped Kinski write those dismissive rants simply to sell more copies of the autobiography, to better serve those readers who are hungry only for scornful prose. "A rumor cannot be eliminated by truth," the director explained. "You can only kill it by an even wilder rumor."[17]

Perhaps it is because of these kinds of embellishments that Herzog has stated, "I do not make films or features. My films are something else." With regard to fiction and nonfiction, he said, "I do not see the borderline. It's very blurred and things in my films are partially staged."[18] Occasionally lines are provided to the real-life characters of his films. In *The White Diamond*, a stoic villager in Guyana is perched at the edge of a dramatic and inspiring waterfall. In the interview, he conjures the sentiment, "I cannot hear what you say for the thunder that you are." Such a poetic declaration seems more fitting for one of Herzog's operas or narrative films and, indeed, the line actually came from *Cobra Verde*, one of his own fictional films.

Whether presenting his films as fact or fiction, Herzog says, "In both cases, I am a storyteller."[19] This statement seems peculiar for a man whose career has been so dedicated to the genre of documentaries, though Herzog prefers not to call them that. "Facts do not interest me much. Facts are for accountants. Truth creates illumination."[20] In response to critics who have questioned the practice of directing the actions of his nonfiction subjects, Herzog has explained that people sometimes have to become actors to better play themselves. While the real events and people of his documentaries are sometimes embellished, it is interesting to note that the events of his fictional narrative *Fitzcarraldo* were brutally realized without the cinematic effects that any other director would have surely required. "The studio wanted it to be a plastic miniature boat pulled over a garden hill, but I said we will pull a real ship over a real mountain, and it will be a grandiose event in a magnificent opera. I wanted the audience to be able to trust their eyes."[21]

It simply did not occur to a man like Herzog that moving a boat over a mountain is nearly impossible; he seemed to accept the task with the same nonchalance that one might take in just typing the words on the page. Herzog's cavalier style of filmmaking could only have been acquired organically, without knowing how filmmaking is *supposed* to be, but rather how he *wants* it to be. "I personally don't believe in the kind of film schools you find all over the world," he explained.[22] "I never worked as another filmmaker's assistant and I never had any formal training."[23] Perhaps this is why he defies any classification and refuses to follow so many established Hollywood filmmaking practices. This is not in spite of the Hollywood system, but instead is the result of learning to work with the minimum and allowing the ideas and characters, whether fictional or real, to be the centerpiece of the production. This minimalist approach has baffled some, like those who worked on his film *Rescue Dawn*, a retelling of an American pilot's escape from a Vietnamese prison camp. The first assistant director lamented, "For a man of his age, it's a very . . . raw talent. It's more like an eighteen-year-old running into the forest."[24]

For Herzog, however, the basic approach to storytelling is a way to shed all the unnecessary aspects of production. He claimed that to produce a film, one only needs a car, a phone and a type-writer, a fitting arsenal for someone whose self-taught profession began by reading a fifteen-page entry on filmmaking in the encyclopedia. The simplicity of his method is more fitting for a man who works on modest productions. Even his demeanor and tone hardly match the galvanized persona many attribute to the eccentric German director.

One can only wonder how Herzog has maintained such a calm exterior amid the crushing difficulties he has faced in filmmaking. Perhaps it is the toll of time that leaves him weathered and worn, like the immovable isthmus conquered in *Fitzcarraldo*. Or perhaps this peaceful soul is half of a duality that came into existence as a result of joining the sane and insane, Werner Herzog and Klaus Kinski.

The Good Soldier of Cinema

The single most brutal force in the punishing South American location of *Fitzcarraldo* was not a mountain or the heat, but rather a man: Klaus Kinski. Herzog's first memory of the actor was watching him perform in the film *Children, Mother, and the General*. It was a simple yet unforgettable scene for Herzog, in which Kinski, playing a soldier, is asleep with his head down on a table, and then is suddenly awakened. "The way he wakes up will forever stay in my memory,"[25] Herzog recalled. "It was a decisive factor in my professional life." Despite this past fascination, Kinski was not an original cast member in *Fitzcarraldo*. American actor Jason Robards was slated to play the lead, with a young Mick Jagger cast as the sidekick Wilbur. The film found its original inspiration in a real rubber baron, Carlos Fermin Fitzcarrald, who attempted a similar feat of crossing a large tract of land with a boat, though he had the foresight to use a much smaller craft and to dismantle it first. "There's really very little known about this authentic figure," Herzog said. "He was a rubber baron in this area, very average. It's the stupid, uninteresting story of a man who exploited a vast area. And once he moved a boat over an isthmus. That's about all."[26]

Before Herzog had even settled upon this real character as an inspiration for the film, his earliest motivation to tell the story came during a drive along the Brittany coast. He came across a commune beside the Gulf of Morbihan called Carnac, where vast rows of large stones stand perfectly straight. There are over 3,000 of these prehistoric menhirs, a lasting creation of the pre-Celtic people of the area. Those who have grown up around them are familiar with the popular legend that they are the remnants of a Roman legion turned to stone by the sorcerer Merlin. The rocks extend for miles like carefully sown rows of crops, some weighing hundreds of tons. When Herzog discovered that there was no definitive scientific answer for how these formations were created under the primitive conditions of the Neolithic period, he became intrigued with the challenge of working out in his mind how it could have been achieved. He mapped out a process by which he believed the stones could be moved and made to stand straight using a series of ditches, ramps, ropes and levers. This very type of problem-solving and engineering would later be critical to the equally anguishing task of pulling a boat over a mountain. However, Herzog would have far fewer than the 2,000 men he calculated would be needed to realize a configuration like what he saw that night on the Brittany coast.

It is questionable if the first serious turn for the worse in the production of the film was Robards's departure or the subsequent decision to replace him with Kinski. After only six weeks of shooting, Robards fell ill with amoebic dysentery and had no choice but to return home to the states for recovery, with no hope of rejoining the picture. That six-week span represented 40 percent of what was to be the completed film. The frenetic search for a solution to this problem worsened when Mick Jagger, who sup- posedly helped Herzog write the script, was forced to abandon the project as well due to previous commitments with the Rolling Stones. The two actors likely didn't miss the rugged lifestyle to which they had to adapt, living in tents without electricity or any means of communication other than weekly trips to Equitos to receive mail and telexes. Robards's agent, Clifford Stevens, pointed to these conditions as an explanation of the actor's illness. "It was a hardship condition right in the jungle, on the Amazon River bank," he said. "It was unhygienic. The place was rife with insects and mosquitoes."[27] For Herzog, the loss of Mick Jagger was an enormous setback in the film. He believed the musician had such a unique and singular talent as an actor that his role could not be recast, only eliminated entirely. "Losing Mick was, I think, the biggest loss I have ever experienced as a film director."[28]

While nearly half of the film had been shot, the entire pro- duction had already consumed more time than any completed film would require. Herzog had worked painstakingly for over three years in the preproduction phase, building the ships as well as a camp equipped to host the 6,000 extras and crew members employed for the film. Now, he was left without any lead actors. After such turmoil in shooting the first half of the film, he was only just ready to begin, but not before a replacement for the lead role could be found.

This person, of course, would be Kinski, a perfect fit, albeit with a decidedly imperfect temperament. It is difficult to imagine anyone else in a role that required braving the unforgiving jungle, performing a profoundly bedeviled character and surviving the ferocity of indigenous tribes. Born in 1926, Kinski grew up in poverty in Poland. While living in Berlin, he was drafted into the military toward the end of World War II. He shortly abandoned his rank, a fitting precedent for a man whom Herzog has claimed left an endless path of broken contracts during his film career. He found a home in the regional theaters in Berlin, occasionally performing one-man shows. He began acting in films in 1948, and by 1960, he acted in at least one film each year for the rest of his career.

It is unclear where the irksome tyrant he often portrays ends and where the real Kinski begins. His bizarre offscreen behavior seemed to promote the caricature he cultivated for himself, but was it real, or was it the remnants of his fictional personas? Excerpts from his autobiography seem to reveal that he had a greater understanding of how others viewed his complicated personality than most people assumed. Some passages intentionally indulge the reader in curiously malicious high jinks. "Once when I was asleep I pissed on my sister because I dreamed she was a tree," he wrote. In another section, he admitted, "I believe there is no stench that I haven't stunk of."[29]

In a review of the autobiography, Alex Ross wrote that while reading the work, "it becomes an interesting game to guess at the real feelings behind this Kinski-esque character called Kinski."[30] Of course, we know from Herzog's own admission that much of Kinski's anger toward him was for show. One can only assume Kinski returned the favor by writing equally fictitious rants about himself. Whether the man Kinski is everything we see, or just a kaleidoscopic representation of all his roles, he was a natural fit to play Fitzcarraldo. Herzog briefly nurtured the notion of playing the lead role himself if all other options proved unsuccessful, so when offered the role, Kinski accepted with bravado. Over a bottle of champagne with Herzog in a New York City hotel, Kinski proclaimed, "I knew it, Werner! I knew I would be Fitzcarraldo! You are not going to play the part because I am much better than you."[31] One problem had been solved, and several more appeared to take its place.

The natural environment of the location was challenging enough without the equally dangerous human elements that threatened the safety of the cast and crew. It was soon discovered that the region where they would be shooting was the epicenter of an escalating border war between Peru and Ecuador. "Has bad luck taken up residence with us? I feel a kind of aimless gratitude for every nondescript day that passes without some disaster. The sound of woodcutting echoes from far off through the jungle. The river, now quiet, is withdrawing more and more into itself," Herzog wrote.[32] Herzog and his crew had to navigate strategically around the various camps of soldiers. To further complicate the dynamics, there were several oil companies that had opportunistically seized on oil fields, building pipelines throughout the territory of the indigenous Indian population. Herzog took the precaution of requesting permission from the locals before setting up camp, but this seemed to do little for the PR of the film. Herzog believed that many media outlets had unfairly targeted his project. "The media forgot all about the war and the oil because we had real media appeal for them."[33] But Herzog defended his practices. "A human rights group sent a commission down to the area and concluded that there had not been one single violation. I had the feeling the wilder and more bizarre the legends were, the faster they would wither away, and this is what happened. After about two years of being criminalized by the press, the whole thing just faded away."[34]

Without question the political situation was unstable. Writer Brad Prager explored the situation faced by the production team, explaining, "The Peruvian government had been encouraging settlers to move into the jungle, and lumber and oil interests were also encroaching on that part of the forest, all of which 'made the Aguaruna Indians see every stranger as a threat.' Although Herzog reached an agreement with the local Aguarunas, who were willing to work with him, a newly-established tribal council decided to set itself at odds with the film's production. According to Herzog, the council 'was merely trying to make a name for itself' by blaming them for having built an oil pipeline and 'generally being responsible for the military presence.'"[35] These problems were man-made, and thus were only half of the struggle for Herzog and the crew amid a forbidding jungle.

Before an attempt could be made to hoist the boat, they had to clear the thick terrain of vines and brush to provide a smooth surface for the ship to drag across. Much of this was done by hand with machetes and chainsaws. One particularly brutal event took place during this phase of the production. As Herzog described, "Once, a lumberman was bitten by a snake while cutting a tree. This only happened once in three years, with hundreds of woodcutters in the jungle who always worked barefoot with their chainsaws. . . . Suddenly this chuchupe struck the man twice. This was the most dangerous snake of all. It only takes a few minutes before cardiac arrest occurs. He dropped the saw and thought about it for five seconds; then he grabbed the saw again and cut off his foot. It saved his life, because the camp and serum was twenty minutes away."[36]

While Herzog has asserted many times that the element of danger in the process of his filmmaking was eliminated as much as possible, it is doubtless that a story as dramatic as this would conjure terrifying possibilities. The director has maintained, "I am a professional person. Others would not do what I do, but I am trying to be the good soldier of cinema."[37] Given Herzog's adherence to reality, it is no surprise that the making of this film is explored more frequently than the narrative of the picture. While the result of his efforts is a fictional tale, *Fitzcarraldo* is a film that could have only been realized through experiencing it head-on, as if the process of filmmaking is the real pursuit, and the final cut a mere by-product. For a man who has spoken frequently of the "ecstatic truth," one can only assume that the production means as much as the premiere. Perhaps *Fitzcarraldo*, more than any of his other films, is the best example of how the process has come to overshadow the story. Herzog must have had some intimation of this truth prior to embarking on such an adventure, given his decision to commission Les Blank to make a documentary film of this brutal undertaking, which was ultimately a four-year struggle.

Only Ashes Left of Me

By joining the film well into production, Kinski had already avoided significant difficulties. Earlier, one of the crew camps had become the target of a hostile attack by armed Indians. The crew fled the camp, traveling down river as their rustic living quarters burned to the ground. The task of finding a new shooting location involved analyzing aerial shots with the assistance of pilots and geographers familiar with the area. "Apparently things are looking very good, except that the whole situation might collapse from one moment to the next," wrote Herzog early in the production.[38] The challenge that faced him was so unique that it truly required a review of nearly all of the jungle before the right conditions were found. The story called for Fitzcarraldo to traverse a narrow section of land where two rivers bend in toward each other, nearly touching. This isthmus had to consist of a small mountain over which Herzog and his crew could drag a steamboat. The distance and slope of the land could not be too inconsequential or too great. For this reason the camp—the civilization they knew—was a distant outpost from where they would shoot much of the film.

These varied and distant locations meant having to shoot the film using three steamboats, one of which would be used exclusively for pulling over the mountain. The others were to be used for shots on the river. The original steamboat was a massive relic constructed in 1902 in Glasgow and found in Colombia on one of the Amazon tributaries. For a portion of its life, the ship was used as a war vessel against Colombia and would later be the very location a peace treaty was signed.

One of the only professional pieces of equipment used in production was a bulldozer, which cleared a path for the boat to be dragged upon. The machine consumed 150 gallons of fuel a day and, like so many other necessities on set, the gasoline had to be flown in. When it malfunctioned, which was not an uncommon setback, spare parts had to be flown in from Miami. The waiting time was occasionally prolonged when they received the wrong replacement parts. Even when the bulldozer was fully operational, bulldozing the trail was frequently halted by heavy downpours, which sometimes even washed away previous work, thus further prolonging shooting.

These long stretches of waiting became taxing to the Indians hired to work on the film. The camp they inhabited during production was initially designed for three months of living. This length of time doubled, and soon it began to take a serious toll on the workers, as they were left with little reprieve from the grind-

ing labor of reshaping the landscape. In an isolated location without even a soccer ball to distract them, the Indians became restless. It was eventually decided to bring prostitutes to the
male-dominated camp to alleviate tensions. On this decision Herzog remarked, "Here it is standard expectation and standard
behavior and somehow the . . . I don't know . . . the jungle sweats
it out. It's not even obscene."[39]

While the jungle sweated out the turmoil, Herzog and his cast
and crew did the same. The physical stress was as evident on the
massive pulley system as it was on the 700 Indians who worked in
groups to slowly turn the large wooden posts that moved the
steamboat inch by inch. The mountain originally had a gradient of
60 percent; the reshaping of the land reduced this to 40 percent,
but this was still double what the Brazilian engineer had designed
the system to withstand. There was no reference against which to
measure success, and there was no field manual to guide them—
the challenge was completely unique. Each day the boat moved
a little farther up the one-hundred-foot-wide path they had carved
for themselves.

At times the story of the film appears to be based on the conflict of man versus nature, but at other moments, it is the tale of
a character who is embattled with himself and his own delusions.
Herzog is certainly no stranger to such outward and inward trials,
even in his personal life. In 1974 Herzog had learned that a close
friend, Lotte Eisner, a French-German film critic and historian,
was seriously ill. She had suffered a massive stroke and was
believed by many to be very close to death. For Herzog, it was a
loss he simply would not allow. Herzog described her as "probably
my most important mentor." She was "very supportive from early
on, and at the time I received the call, I knew it was too early, she
should not—she *must* not die."[40] Instead of booking a flight, he

endeavored to travel on foot from Munich to her Paris apartment, hoping, perhaps believing, that she would live long enough for him to complete the trek during the bitter winter months. Herzog recalled, "I just would not let her die because I came walking one million steps and somehow I knew she would, she would be out of hospital and she would be alive."[41] Equipped with only a bundle of clothing, a map and a compass, he set off to see her. On the way he slept wherever he could find shelter, in abandoned buildings or farms. The walk was a supreme gesture of friendship, but reading Herzog's description of the journey invites notions of solitude and experiences that border on the metaphysical. "When I am walking I fall deep into dreams, I float through fantasies and find myself inside unbelievable stories. I literally walk through whole novels and films and football matches. I do not even look where I am stepping, but I never lose my direction. When I come out of a big story I find myself twenty-five or thirty kilometers further on. How I got there I do not know."[42]

When he finally arrived she was still alive. She continued to live for several more years, until one day she remarked to him that she had had enough, that she was ready. In jest, he told her that he would lift his spell off of her. She died a few weeks later.

For Herzog, the brutal cold of his long walk was likely a distant, perhaps even nostalgic, memory as he worked under the hot sun of the Amazon jungle. The water level dropped toward the end of the rainy season, causing the motor on the back of the boat to lift partially out of the water, leaving it with insufficient force to move the boat. As production shrugged forward, Herzog seemed to become increasingly distant from the organized world of production schedules and technical protocols. Interviews with the director on set indicated this sense of detachment. "If I believed in the devil, I would say the devil was right here and is still right here," he said.[43] Even Kinski's thundering temper was a muted squeak among the rising cacophony of jungle sounds. Listless, the actor remarked, "You can't go anywhere, you can't go, you can't escape this fucking stinking camp."[44] The Indians did not like Kinski any more than some of the other crew members did, who had come to resent the way his childish rage exacerbated an already difficult situation. "The Indians offered to kill Kinski for me," Herzog revealed. "They would have killed him undoubtedly if I had wanted it. I at once regretted that I held the Indians back from their purpose."[45] The anger some of the Indians felt toward Kinski was the result of his tirades and insubordination on set, which held everyone back. "I refuse to do anything unless I consider it right. So I can at least partly save the movie from being wrecked by Herzog's lack of talent."[46] On the set of *Aguirre: The Wrath of God*, Kinski's insubordination nearly cost him his life at the hands of Herzog himself. Herzog recalled his frustration and blinding rage when the actor insisted, "No, I'm leaving now." Herzog would not allow it. "I told him I had a rifle and by the time he'd reach the next bend there'd be eight bullets in his head and the ninth one would be mine. He screamed for the police like a madman. . . . He was very disciplined during the last days of shooting. The beast had been domesticated after all."[47]

Though Kinski remained safe from these threats, some of the Indians who were extras in the film were not as lucky. While the water levels continued to fall, many of the local Indians had to travel farther to find food, which led to disputes over fishing holes. A group of Amahuaca Indians attacked a man and a woman, shooting an arrow through the man's neck and three arrows into the woman's stomach. The hospital was too far away to reach quickly and safely. Instead, the production team helped treat them on a kitchen table, and both survived. Many other events like this—including a plane crash involving people traveling to the production, which left five in critical condition and one person paralyzed—contributed to the film's reputation as a wildly reckless and dangerous project.

For many years after the completion of the movie, Herzog faced scornful rumors about these disasters that were very much out of his control, though he took responsibility for a less serious accident on the set, which he still laughs at today. An assistant cameraman was placed on a rock surrounded by rushing water in order to film the boat traversing the rapids. Herzog and the remaining crew steered the boat downriver, made it through the tight turn around the rock and returned to camp. The following morning they realized that they had completely forgotten to pick up the crew member on the rock. Herzog, of course, returned in a boat to retrieve him.

Problems with less clear solutions continued to hinder the already sluggish production. Once the water level had dropped considerably, the ship became lodged on the bottom of the river. There was no choice but to wait for the rainy season to return and lift the boat off the sand. In the meantime, the central images of the film remained incomplete as Herzog struggled to pull the other boat over the mountain. His growing frustrations were evident in his observations of the jungle around this time. "I see fornication and asphyxiation and choking and fighting for survival and growing and rotting away."[48] Herzog eventually came to the realization that heavier equipment would be needed, as well as a new crew to move the boat. He recruited a group from Lima to help put an end to his picture.

In November 1981, four years after preproduction began, Herzog and his team finally shot the last scenes of *Fitzcarraldo*. The worst, it seemed, was behind him. Yet, there still lay ahead the festering rumors and critical reviews that would, in time, give the picture a different life. Some reviewers saw little merit in the picture or the dramatic efforts taken to tell the story. A *Washington Post* review dismissed the picture as inconsequential, saying of the boat movement, "The awful truth is that it's a cheated image that has inescapably ugly implications. There's nothing exalting about the thought of a real army of laborers, rather than a monster bulldozer, budging several tons of boat. It's an epic illusion that doesn't work and isn't worth the appalling effort."[49] Regardless of Herzog's own feelings about the final product, it is clear the experience had taken an enormous toll. "Nobody on this earth will convince me to be happy about this," he lamented.[50] Shortly after the release he explained, "A film like this costs a lot to make, I don't mean in terms of money. There is much on my shoulders that I have to carry with me forever."[51] Perhaps even then, he knew that this film would always remain the most difficult picture of his life. "I will not do [a picture like] this film as my next film," he admitted. "There would be only ashes left of me."[52]

Vicious accusations continued to circulate. Some believed that the Indians who assisted in the production were treated improperly. Herzog maintained that the description of the work to the Indians was always clear and that they were paid appropriate wages for their efforts. The payment they received was supposedly close to double what they could have expected from a lumber company.

The making of the film was discussed just as frequently as the narrative on the screen. But, on many occasions, Herzog resisted the inquiries of academics and film historians. "Concerning the process behind the making, it doesn't help to know anything about it. The making of the film requires a lot of discipline. . . . The procedure is sometimes very banal, very stupid, very technical and is filled with discipline. It's a struggle with banalities in order to save something that stays in your heart and in your soul for a long time."[53] He has explained that these inquiries of "Why make this film?" or "What does it mean?" are often useless. "I do not like introspection, I don't like to look at myself."[54] To better illustrate the sincerity of his message, he revealed, "I swear to God I do not know the color of my eyes." Despite the numerous analyses of the production, as well as Herzog's own revelations about those years in the jungle, the director asserted, "I believe nothing will ever depict properly and adequately the work on *Fitzcarraldo*."[55]

Herzog worked with Kinski on only one more film, *Cobra Verde* in 1987. Afterward, Herzog and Kinski decided it would be their final collaboration. Herzog explained that Kinski's seemingly interminable energy finally fizzled out. "He burned away like a comet," Herzog said. "Afterwards he was ashes." Their time together was over. "This is what I sensed, and he himself said something similar," Herzog remembered. "He said, 'We can go no further.'"[56] In 1989 Klaus Kinski died of a heart attack. He had starred in over one hundred films.

Herzog has continued to direct an increasingly diverse collection of narratives and documentaries. His experience and trials in the jungle are likely a memory that is both distant and close, quieted and unreconciled, real and imagined. Speaking of the unforgiving jungle location, he said, "It is the harmony of overwhelming and collective murder. . . . I love it against my better judgment."[57] To love something against his better judgment certainly describes his relationship with Kinski, as well as that with his work, with the past, with truth and fiction, and with all the stories that undoubtedly lay ahead for him.

6

It's Good to Be Kim

Pulgasari

Vacant

I N THE NORTH KOREAN CAPITAL of Pyongyang, a 105-story concrete building dominates the skyline. The pyramid structure of the Ryugyong Hotel rises to a point of 1,083 feet, achieving the distinction of the twenty-second tallest skyscraper in the world. The hotel has 3,000 rooms and 3,000 vacancies; it has never booked a single reservation and likely never will.

Construction began in 1987 and stopped in 1992, and though the outside shell appears to be complete, the building is without windows, plumbing or any discernable lighting. Little is known about the mysterious structure, and even less is spoken about it within North Korea. Some people have speculated that flawed structural designs or inadequate building materials were responsible for the abrupt halt to the construction, but the most likely cause was insufficient funds.

What remains just as perplexing is the need for a massive hotel in a communist country, which attracts and allows so few tourists. This has led many to conclude that the project is a largely ego-driven endeavor—an attempt to overshadow an imposing 73-story hotel completed in Singapore in 1986. Others have said the original impetus was a desire to draw tourists during the 1988 Olympic Games in Seoul.

Above the seven rotating restaurants that form the pinnacle of the Ryugyong Hotel, a single rusty crane remains perched, echoing the days of construction. Though the structure is frequently airbrushed from photographs of the Pyongyang skyline, the building is clearly visible from all vantage points in the city. The government may attempt to attract foreign investment to complete the project in the future, but for now its fate remains unknown.

Over the years the hotel has come to represent the secretive, enigmatic and wildly impulsive practices of the communist regime in physical form. Some journalists have likened the monstrosity to a piece of cinematic science fiction come to life. Perhaps this association is especially fitting for a country whose ruler is so enraptured by the spectacle of film.

As a portly five-foot-three-inch man, Kim Jong Il has a penchant for the grandeur of structures like the Ryugyong Hotel. In an attempt to bolster his image as a living god, he has spent billions on monuments designed to commemorate his stature, as well as his father's. By the late 1980s, over 34,000 monuments to Kim Jong Il had been completed at his demand. But even all these structures could not satiate Kim Jong Il's appetite for larger-than-life exhibitions. He was especially taken with the kind of dramatic images provided by his vast personal collection of movies, reported to consist of 10,000 to 15,000 titles. Within this library, he owns every Oscar-winning movie, every installment of the *Friday the 13th* series, all of James Bond's adventures and every *Rambo* movie.

Perhaps high-concept action cinema colors the way he sees the world outside the insulated cult of personality that surrounds him. The goal of this cult is to deify a ruler, making him impervious to the criticism of others, and to inextricably link his leadership with the preservation of the state. Kim Jong Il has strived to achieve a reputation of supreme existence through the boasted achievements of impossible feats. As a student at the Kim Il Sung University, he was said to have penned over 1,000 books. It is this magnanimous existence and larger-than-life persona that has led to his fondness for the towering scale of the cinema.

His methods of ruling North Korea mirror the responsibilities of a movie director, actor and producer all rolled into one. The government officials and citizens of his country are compelled to satisfy his every whim at any given time. One of Kim Jong Il's former personal chefs recalled the lavish, alcohol-fueled parties in which the guests were not permitted to go to sleep until Kim Jong Il turned in for the night. "It was torture for them," he remembered.[1]

These parties are said to have sometimes lasted several days, a relentless pursuit of hedonism. Without regard to cost or consequence, the fleeting desires of Kim Jong Il must always be met. Many of his exploits are realized not only at the cost of fortunes, but at the cost of lives, such as the millions of people who have starved beneath the bronze sculptures of his likeness.

Yet, even the resilience of his rule cannot bring his wildest fantasies to life. For this he has the movies. As with all other forms of art, Kim Jong Il demands that movies produced within North Korea promote his communist agenda and his regime. Though the concrete tomb of architectural ambition known as the Ryugyong Hotel would remain an immovable reminder of state failures and irrationality, with the magic of cinema Kim Jong Il could edit, dub over or reshoot an unsuccessful past.

Something even bigger and more awe-inspiring would replace the looming hotel in the public consciousness. It would not rely upon flawed blueprints or crumbling cement, but instead the more durable and permanent nature of a legend. Just as fantastic stories formed the basis of Kim Jong Il's stature, a similar phenomenon would be used to propel the tale of his proposed movie idea: the epic legend of a fourteenth-century monster who ravages the countryside and grows larger with the consumption of iron. The landscape and skyline would no longer be interrupted by a forgotten building, but instead a colossal beast.

The monster would serve as a Marxist allegory for the dangers of capitalism. After helping the peasants fulfill their revolutionary destiny, the monster would turn on them and destroy them. Japan had *Godzilla,* and Kim Jong Il would have his monster too. All that remained was to find a talented director and a willing host of extras, but of course, these things posed no problem for a man of such means. Soon the viewing public would know of Kim Jong Il the director. They would know of *Pulgasari*.

It's Good to Be Kim

North Korean hagiography tells of Kim Jong Il's birth in 1942 occurring in a cabin on Mount Paektu, the highest point in Korea. This divine location intimated that Kim Jong Il was born not as a common man, but as a unique leader emerging from the sacred chrysalis of heaven. The glorious event of his birth is said to have been foretold by a swallow and celebrated by the appearance of a double rainbow and a star in the sky. He would become known as the last of the "three generals of Mount Paektu"; the first two generals were his mother and father.

Of course, many historians tell a more humble, unofficial version of his birth. A year earlier, in 1941, he was born in a Soviet military camp in Siberia where his father and a small crew of communist guerrillas were hiding from the Japanese.

The story of Kim Jong Il as the "Star of Paetku" was only the first thread in a string of fantastic tales that have been told about the leader. As the stories continue, the people of North Korea are presented with a dynamic picture of a man whose otherworldly accomplishments point to celestial origins.

However, while this cult of personality includes many false proclamations, his wild lifestyle is very much a reality. One of Kim's sushi chefs, who goes by the pseudonym Kenji Fujimoto, described his stockpile of 10,000 bottles of wine and fine cognac. His taste for cuisine is just as particular, especially when it comes to pizza. In 1999 his agents arranged for two Italian chefs to come to North Korea to create a top-of-the-line gourmet pizza kitchen and to train Kim Jong Il's personal chefs in its preparation.

Ermanno Furlanis, part-time chef at the Pizza Institute in northern Italy, remembered that the call came in the middle of the night. The head chef of a high-end hotel was on the other end telling Furlanis that foreign diplomats had contacted him looking for experts in the culinary field to present demonstrations "in a communist country in the Far East."[2]

In Pyongyang, Furlanis taught his pizza-making techniques to three military officers. They watched with the attentiveness of medical students witnessing a surgical procedure and took copious notes. One of them even asked to count the number of olives and measure the distance between them. "He looked totally serious," Furlanis recalled.

For three weeks during the training, he was an addition to the permanent arsenal of 2,000 maids, doctors, gardeners, masseurs, dancing troupes, bodyguards, cooks and valets that surround Kim Jong Il. One section of this entourage consists of three women in their early twenties who shadow his every move and are replaced every six months. He enjoys many outsized luxuries around his palace, including golf courses, fully stocked hunting grounds and horse stables. The great distance between these areas requires travel in one of his one hundred imported S500 class Mercedes Benz limousines. He tracks the time between his activities with the help of his $2.6 million collection of watches from Switzerland. Though he could remain comfortably nestled in his dictatorial lifestyle at home, his reach for opulence extends to all corners of the world. He has acquired the services of Turkish belly dancers, Russian pop singers, professional wrestlers from America and Romanian knife throwers.

However, his darker desires go beyond simple entertainment. In an attempt at misdirection, Kim Jong Il labeled his insatiable sexual appetite as "The Project to Guarantee the Longevity of the Great Leader and the Dear Leader." This "project" consisted of a task force charged with the duty of locating 2,000 girls to audition for the "satisfaction team" and the "happiness team," as well as a group of singers and dancers. Kim Jong Il made his final pick of the top fifty girls to form these three groups.

From the first stories of Mount Paektu, Kim Jong Il has taken great pains to shroud any hint of his own commonness. He builds a mysterious existence by keeping out of sight. Author Gordon G. Chang writes in his 2006 publication *Nuclear Showdown: North Korea Takes on the World* that Kim Jong Il "has only ever said six words to the North Korean people in a public setting. During that occasion, Kim uttered, 'Glory to the people's heroic military!'" Chang calls him "the ultimate 'behind-the-scenes operator,' the global leader who most resembles the Wizard of Oz."

Throughout his life, Kim Jong Il was very much in the shadow of his revered father, Kim Il Sung. Yet, he began making strategic movements toward greater power during the twilight years of his father's rule. Until his father's death in 1994, Kim Jong Il carefully orchestrated all reports to his father by presenting him with false notions regarding the condition of North Korea, just as he would do to so many citizens later in life. Lee Young-guk, a bodyguard, said that when Kim Jong Il spoke to his father, "He would be as obsequious as one can imagine," but "behind his back he would do what he wanted."[3] Jasper Becker also relates the account of Dr. Park Young-ho, a member of the Institute for Unification in Seoul, who said, "Kim Jong Il had lied to his father about the true state of the economy for years." It seems to logically follow that Kim Jong Il would have a vested interest in the success of his country, even if only for the purpose of continuing his lifestyle of conspicuous consumption. Yet, as so many starved, his spending continued at astronomical rates, plunging the country into further despair.

Though it appears he has always had a fondness for movies, at some juncture this fondness mutated into a determination to actually create them. It offered another world for him to command. Even if the worlds and narratives of his celluloid creations were fictitious, they were still of his making, and thus they would be very real to him, certainly real enough to fit within the equally absurd features of his "real" life. While filmmaking would do nothing to stop the deterioration of North Korea, it may have provided a realm in which his delusions would be confined to sound stages and tiny flickering frames. The words he never spoke to his people would be spoken through the dialogue of his actors and his flimsy cautionary tales. Money, as usual, would be no object.

Kim Jong Il had been interested in film for some time, and he managed to collect his thoughts on the craft in a 329-page book titled *On the Art of the Cinema*. Some of the chapter titles in this 1973 publication demonstrate an unsettling parallel to his methods of rule, such as one that reads "The Director Is the Commander of the Creative Group." His practice of censoring information is reflected in another chapter called, "The Secret of Directing Lies in Editing." In the latter half of the book Kim Jong Il seems to finally abandon all pretense of artistic discussion for more political subjects, like those discussed in the chapter, "Be Loyal to the Party and Prove Yourselves Worthy of the Trust It Places in You." Throughout the text, his musings swing wildly between insights into filmmaking and his promotion of the communist model.

At times, however, his remarks on the artistry and abstract nature of films are unexpectedly pertinent. He writes, "In works of art and literature, as in everything else, form and content are in dialectical relationship. Just as form is inconceivable without content, so is content without form. The content determines and restricts the form and the form follows and expresses the content."[4]

In other chapters, however, he cannot help but drift back toward his dictatorial communist agenda. In the chapter "Directing for the Cinema," he explains, "The task set before the cinema today is one of contributing to people's development into true communists and assisting in the revolutionizing and remodeling of the whole of society on the working-class pattern."[5] For Kim Jong Il, the movies, like all else, are yet another weapon in his arsenal against the capitalist form. "In the capitalist system of filmmaking the 'director' carries that title, but in fact the right of supervision and control over film production is entirely in the hands of the tycoons of the filmmaking industry who have the money, whereas the directors are nothing but their agents."[6] This characterization of directors as agents of a higher power seems particularly hypocritical when written by a dictator who has held rigid command over all films produced in his country. *Washington Post* writer Peter Carlson reported that Kim Jong Il once commissioned a staggering one-hundred-part serial on the history of North Korea. Kongdan Oh, a Korean scholar, said, "Kim Jong Il can claim credit—I wrote it, I directed it—but it is lies, of course."[7]

Yet, in a sheltered communist regime, where is the Dear Leader to find the suitable directing and acting talent needed to realize the dream projects so exhaustively penned in his writings on cinema? Even more problematic, how could the capable talents outside North Korea ever be convinced to journey into the dark reaches of the dictator's land? His world was not one of contracts, business luncheons or negotiations. The world he inhabited was a creation wholly his own, and any directors or actors employed would be no more difficult to position and control than the lighting on the set. Yet, the country had been ravaged by famine, and thus there was a scarcity of experts at his disposal. If other countries were to recognize North Korea's place in the world of cinema, he would need the kind of professionals who were already established in their profession. The man who had everything was suddenly in need.

If foreign luxuries like food, cars and watches could be imported, then why not a respected director and admired actress? Even to a man as myopic as Kim Jong Il, it was clear that talent like this would not come willingly. Therefore, a plot was devised to kidnap the revered South Korean actress Choi Eun-hee and her husband, the well-known South Korean director Shin Sang-ok. Kim Jong Il would not blindly venture into the industry of filmmaking; instead the industry would come to him. For Kim Jong Il, there were award-winning productions to look forward to, but for Choi Eun-hee and Shin Sang-ok, a nightmare was about to begin.

"Shall We Make Mr. Shin One of Our Regular Guests?"

Though most Americans have never heard of Shin Sang-ok, his contribution to cinema is immeasurable. With seventy-two titles under his direction, his career was nothing short of prolific. However, his impact on the craft goes beyond mere volume. He was the first Korean director to use and harness the impact of the 135 mm telephoto lens. His technical milestones also include the first attempt at synchronized sound in the film *King's Father* in the 1960s. His studio, the Shin Film Company, produced approximately 300 films, which was made possible in part through his direction of approximately two films a year from 1960 to 1970. His distribution company, Seoul Films, was a steady conduit through which these films reached the public.

Shin Sang-ok was the antithesis of Kim Jong Il. He was a man who extended offerings of art to the people instead of drawing them inward to himself. For Shin Sang-ok, the ultimate goal, as well as benefit, of the cinema was the audience's enjoyment. In fact, he believed that "the greatest movie is the one that attracts the widest [audience]. Naturally, a director is often tempted to show off his talents in his films. But for me, pleasing as many people as I can must come first."[8]

As a successful genre director, he favored casting well-known actors and actresses in his pictures. One performer particularly close to his heart was Choi Eun-hee, a venerated actress who became his wife. In adherence to the Hollywood model, Shin remarked, "If you don't use stars in Hollywood, you'll face disadvantages in marketing the film."[9] Yet, Shin pushed the boundaries in his work, often presenting his performers with roles that challenged social norms. One such film was *A Flower in Hell* (1958) in which Choi Eun-hee plays Sonya, a prostitute to American soldiers. Film critic Hong Sung-nam described the brazen character of Sonya as an "irresistibly poisonous figure" who "obtains power from her fatal sexuality."[10] These traits were a far cry from the gender roles to which the audience of the time was accustomed. Hong recognized this, saying, "Her usual persona of the endlessly patient traditional Korean woman echoes discordantly through her personification of a femme fatale like Sonya." This theme of strong female characters entrenched in a battle for autonomy continued with other performances by Choi in films like *The Evergreen Tree* in 1961. She quickly established herself as a dynamic element in the movement to reconstruct the image of women in Korea. As film critic Kwak Hyun-Ja explained, "She becomes a textual site where modernity and tradition struggle and negotiate over the status of women at that time."[11] The 1960s marked a triumphant era for Shin, who brought so much social advancement and technical innovation to the screen. Yet, from this height of success, a void rested below.

Shin's status as a legendary director was shaken in the 1970s when his name was the subject of political debate in South Korea. The government of General Park Chung-hee took issue with Shin, who refused to edit his films to meet their demands. In time, he was stripped of his film production license. This proved to be the final straw for the Shin Film Company, already marred by financial failures. His career crumbled and his marriage began to deteriorate. Much like Kim Jong Il, who faced the dilemma of an empty director's chair, Shin, once the master of Korean cinema, faced an empty studio. Shin decided to set his sights on wider markets. If his career could not continue in South Korea, perhaps foreign regions could be tapped. This, in fact, was exactly what happened, but not in the way Shin had hoped.

All concerns about his career were immediately forgotten in 1978, when Choi Eun-hee, who was divorced from Shin by then, suddenly went missing. She had been lured to Hong Kong with the prospect of a potential role and never returned. On January 14, 1978, Shin traveled to Hong Kong to look for her. Little did he know that Kim Jong Il had kidnapped Choi to perform in his films and to lure Shin into a trap. It worked. On July 19, 1978, six months after he began his search, Shin was kidnapped by North Korean agents. Shortly after the kidnapping, newspapers throughout the world featured headlines of the incident. South Korea condemned the act, of course, which further destabilized already faltering relations between the two countries.

Choi's arrival in North Korea after her abduction was as cinematic as any scene in which she had ever acted. She was escorted to the country by ship, and when she disembarked a man stood waiting for her on the dock. He said, "You have suffered a great deal trying to come here. I am Kim Jong Il."[12] Shin's introduction to North Korea was far less welcoming; he was incapacitated with chloroform and immediately held as a prisoner. "Someone suddenly pulled a sack over my head and I couldn't see anything or breathe properly,"Shin remembered.[13] He made many escape attempts, all unsuccessful. In one such attempt Shin got hold of a car and drove to a railway station where he hid among cargo crates, and then made his way into a freight train.[14] He was caught the next day. This seems to have only strengthened Kim Jong Il's resolve. Shin was punished with a four-year detainment at Prison No. 6. The meager diet provided to him consisted of grass, salt and rice. Shin later recalled that he was "tasting bile all the time." This was the darkest time of his imprisonment under Kim Jong Il. "I experienced the limits of human beings," Shin said.[15] He was kept away from his wife during the four years of his confinement.

"Life is Struggle and Struggle is Life," Kim Jong Il wrote in *On the Art of the Cinema*. "A writer who is to serve the people must naturally have a deep interest in their lives, and be quick to recognize the urgent problems which can be used to raise the level of their class consciousness." Without question, Shin and Choi had never before had as deep an interest in their lives as they did when in the seclusion of the Dear Leader's prison.

Kim Jong Il's reasons for keeping the director and his wife confined for so many years remain unclear. Though the imprisonment was perhaps punishment for escape attempts, Shin and his wife were unable to fulfill Kim Jong Il's desire for a better film industry while locked up. Perhaps it was his maniacal wish to manufacture the despair he believed to be so crucial to the development of an artist. He wrote, "A life which develops through intense struggle is the most ennobling and beautiful." This statement stands in stark contrast to the assessment made by Shin of his time spent in confinement. "What a wretched fate,"[16] he recalled.

The confinement was torture for Shin. Failed escape attempts and seclusion were followed by a plummet into depression. Shin tried to starve himself to death, but the guards were given strict orders to force-feed him through a funnel. It was rare for a guard to receive a directive to curtail a prisoner's suicide attempt; they told Shin he must be an important person. The years crawled by as both Shin and Choi shared a dejected existence while never knowing of the other's imprisonment.

Shin began to write letters to Kim Jong Il, begging for help. In a series of protracted apologies to the Dear Leader and his father Kim Il Sung, he attempted to appeal to the dictator's communist sensibilities. Eventually, it worked. After four long years of imprisonment, Shin was released from his cell but was still detained within North Korea under the watchful eye of Kim Jong Il, who was finally ready to produce movies. After Shin's release, Kim hosted a lavish dinner party to reunite Shin and Choi.

The year was 1983. After a four-year separation they now stood face to face in the palace of Kim Jong Il. They didn't know what to say. Finally, Kim instructed, "Well, go ahead and hug each other. Why are you just standing there?"[17] He later suggested that they remarry, but of course in a dictatorship there are no suggestions, only orders, and like any other order, they were obliged to comply. It was yet another chapter in their bizarre life in North Korea. The man who had ordered their capture was now urging Shin and Choi to make believe they were husband and wife again, as if nothing had happened. For Kim, it was all make believe; sometimes even he acknowledged this. Amid the regalement of generals and dancers at the party chanting, "Long live the great leader," Kim simply turned to Shin and said: "Mr. Shin, all that is bogus. It's just pretense."[18] For Shin and Choi, it marked the transition into the next half of their ordeal, but for Kim it was just another party and just two more guests. He enjoyed Shin's company at the celebration and asked his visitors, "Shall we make Mr. Shin one of our regular guests?"[19] The reply didn't matter; Shin and Choi were here to stay. There were movies to be made.

The Steel Beast

Kim insisted he was not responsible for the carelessness and disregard of the government officials who locked up Shin and Choi. He offered an apology for neglecting to see to their release until this late date. His excuse: He had been busy in his office.

After their release, there was no time to waste; Kim was anxious to begin production. The Dear Leader deposited a sum of

$2.5 million in an Austrian account, telling Shin that the funds were at his disposal for the purposes of making films.[20] Some have reported Shin's annual production budget to have been $3 million a year. He was also provided a staff of 700 to assist him in his productions. Producer Kim Jong Il also provided truckloads of pheasants, wild geese and deer for the crew's meals.

The once failing Shin Film was resurrected in Pyongyang, North Korea. Shin and Choi would still face the burden of heavy bureaucracy, inadequate distribution and malfunctioning equipment in the production of their movies. Yet, despite all this, there was finally purpose for Shin and Choi. No longer confined to their cells, they would have challenges to conquer and goals to achieve. They would make movies.

Absurdly, a once-forgotten career had been revived by an inspired dictator. Shin's studio in South Korea was ruined at the hands of meddlesome government officials, and in this new totalitarian setting, he was granted an unexpected amount of artistic freedom. But Kim still insisted on participating in the storyboard conferences. In one of their early meetings, the dictator-producer explained that recent films produced in North Korea were of unsatisfactory quality, perhaps lacking the crucial attributes he had written about ten years earlier in his book. He explained, "The North's filmmakers are just doing perfunctory work. They don't have any new ideas."[21] For a man so enamored with the action genre, these sad narratives were too slow and melodramatic, and it was clear that he wanted less drama and more excitement. He remarked, "All our movies are filled with crying and sobbing. I didn't order them to portray that kind of thing."[22] Now he would make his orders to Shin. There would be no studio system, no production company conglomerates, just Shin, Choi, Kim and an entire country at their disposal.

In this unique situation, Shin was able to orchestrate two, sometimes three, productions at one time, which had been impossible in South Korea. The first picture Shin directed for Kim was *The Emissary Who Did Not Return*. This dramatic story was the first North Korean film to be shot using foreign locations. The plot is based on a play titled *Bloody Conference*, a work thought to be written by Kim Il Sung. The production presented many challenges, including shooting the final scene in only one and a half days with the help of 400 Czech extras.[23]

Shin was dissatisfied with the final cut. In the end, he insisted that Choi's name appear in the credits as director. Despite Shin's misgivings, the film earned the Special Jury Award for best director at the Karlovy Vary International Film Festival. This was exactly the recognition and accolade Kim Jong Il had sought. The film held another distinction that perhaps surpassed the award: It was the first North Korean film to list every crew member's name in the end credits.

Shin introduced several firsts to Kim Jong Il's productions. In an interview with the *Seoul Times*, Shin said of his upcoming film *Runaway*, "I introduced words like 'love' in North Korean film."[24] This word also appeared in the title of his third North Korean film, *Oh My Love*. "I also introduced the first kiss in North Korea in a movie I made with Kim Jong Il," he recalled.[25] These achievements multiplied as the years passed and the productions continued. Then, finally, Shin embarked on what would be his last production in the communist haven: *Pulgasari*.

The script was inspired by a fourteenth-century legend. It tells of a young girl who is saddened by the death of her father, a blacksmith who has crafted a little steel figure of a monster for her and named it Pulgasari. One day, the girl's sewing needle slips, and a drop of her blood falls onto the little figure, bringing it to life. The creature quickly acquires a taste for steel and grows to monolithic proportions on a diet of swords and cannons.

As usual, money was no obstacle for Kim; any expense could be met if it corresponded with his vision. Shin explained, "I never had to worry about money when it came to moviemaking."[26] Kim Jong Il leveraged his astronomical military resources to provide soldiers for the epic battle scenes. With an army of 1 million troops for a population of 22 million people, Kim had a nearly endless supply of soldiers, more per capita than any country in the world.[27] But, despite bottomless funding, the film often exhibits a distinctly low-budget look. The rubbery monster features two bright white human eyes and walks unsteadily on its clawed feet. The creature and the general tone of the movie invite comparisons to the more famous monster Godzilla. Indeed, Kenpachiro Satsuma, the Japanese actor who wore the Godzilla costume in the 1984 film *The Return of Godzilla*, was recruited to portray Pulgasari.

Kim guaranteed safety to numerous production members from Japan who came to help make the movie, and, generally speaking, he remained consistent with the ideals of artistic freedom expressed in his book. As Shin recalled, "Kim Jong Il was very supportive, but he never visited the set."[28] Perhaps the leader of North Korea had more pressing issues to attend to, or maybe he simply believed that a man who had been granted a limitless budget and free rein to direct would never want to leave the glorious confines of North Korea. Kim was content to let Shin do his job. But Choi recalls the Dear Leader's exhaustive attention to detail. "We nicknamed him 'micro-manager.' He pays attention to everything. He keeps track of everything. He is simply amazing."[29] In either case, Shin and Choi were there against their will. There were no contracts, agreements or deals; they would have to stay as long as Kim demanded, which would likely be for good.

Shin's portrayal of the monster's growth in the film exhibits a strong resemblance to Kim Jong Il. Early in the film he is a smaller, modest creature who lumbers around with a protruding belly. His silent meandering through the city crowds is evocative of Kim strolling past the lines of his fully outfitted army. Even Kim himself must have noticed a hint of his likeness in the creature. One day while visiting Choi, he asked, "What do you think of my physique?" Choi, aware that she must tread lightly in response to the dictator's question, made no reply. Kim offered, "Small as a midget's turd, aren't I?"[30]

By the time they began to make *Pulgasari*, Shin and Choi were accustomed to being treated well, though memories of their earlier imprisonment were still fixed in their minds. The charade of Kim the beloved producer, with Shin and Choi his seemingly adoring director and actress, continued. At one point, the couple was required to participate in a press conference professing their willing defection to North Korea.[31]

Despite these forced acts of loyalty in their daily lives, the narrative of *Pulgasari* takes a stance in opposition to many of the values Kim Jong Il represents. At first, the steel monster aids and protects a growing peasant uprising. The guards of the ruling class attack him with swords, but Pulgasari quickly eats all of their weapons and grows even larger. At the victorious moment of the people's overthrow of the government, a problem arises: Pulgasari is still hungry. He turns on the peasants and consumes their tools, thus crippling their ability to build, create and thrive. As Kim explains in *On the Art of the Cinema*, "Following the victory of the socialist revolution, the working-class Party is faced with the task of creating fully-developed communist art and literature." This is the very problem that faced the once victorious villagers.

The story attempts to deliver the cautionary tale that the capitalist structure cannot be sustained and will bring harm to those who believe they will benefit from it. But, as the journalist John Gorenfeld astutely observed, "It is also tempting to read the monster as a metaphor for Kim Il-Sung, hijacking the 'people's revolution' to ultimately serve his purposes." Whatever the intended message, Kim was pleased with the final cut.

From October 1983 to March 1986, Shin and Choi completed seven films and oversaw the production of eleven more. By all outward appearances, Shin's career was at its peak. He made several pictures that would become critical successes. He had the backing of a truly powerful producer. He was remarried to the one and only wife he would ever have. Each day he emerged from his marble-floored office with purpose. But this was not his home, and no matter how long he stayed, it never would be. "I hated communism, but I had to pretend to be devoted to it to escape from this barren republic. It was lunacy."[32] Even a great director and an award-winning actress cannot pretend forever.

The Crossroads

Enchanted by the scale of the *Pulgasari* production, Kim was eager to begin another project. This time the inspiration was Genghis Khan; Kim planned to make a movie about his life and victories. It was the eighth film Shin and Kim would work on together, and they believed it would be their most marketable production. They planned on a widespread distribution overseas and explored the possibility of forming a joint venture with an Austrian film company for this purpose.

By now Kim trusted Shin and Choi, or perhaps he believed they had become addicted to their lifestyle in his palaces and wished never to leave. He allowed them both to travel to Europe in preparation for the movie, though he still insisted that personal escorts shadow the couple. It was not the first time they had been afforded the privilege of leaving North Korea for a production. During a trip to East Berlin, they happened to walk past the U.S. embassy. Choi, careful to avoid drawing attention to herself, tugged on Shin's sleeve in a silent attempt to suggest making an escape. Shin had to ignore it. "What's the matter with you?" he whispered. "I will not make an attempt unless it's 100% certain. If they caught us, we'd be dead."[33] The echoes of his imprisonment still reverberated deeply.

For Choi, the memories must have been just as haunting. During her confinement she was required to attend reeducation classes, part of a protracted attempt to brainwash her about the history of North Korea's "triumphant revolution." She remembered, "I was very unhappy. I did think of suicide but then I thought of my family and how much this would hurt them. It was an awful time."[34] Shin recalled, "If I had known from the start I would rather have been dead. During this time I was very, very depressed. They expected brainwashing to change me."[35] Fortunately, they were both relatively unchanged, and when they boarded a flight to Austria in 1986, it would be the last time they saw their Dear Leader, Kim Jong Il.

Shin and Choi had traveled to Austria to attend a film festival in Vienna. While driving to the event in the company of their escorts, they spied their chance for escape. Choi vividly remembered, "We got to a crossroads where we were supposed to turn left for the festival. Our minders' car was following us about thirty meters behind, but several other cars had got in between them and us. So we told our driver to turn right instead, towards the United States Embassy."[36] Moments later, the escorts radioed the taxi and asked the driver which way he had gone. Before he could answer, Shin and Choi pressed him with a heavy tip and requested that he ignore the radio and continue on his path. When they finally got close to the embassy, there was no place for the car to pull over amid the traffic congestion, so they jumped out and bolted for the doors. "We tried to run as fast as we could, but it felt like we were in some sort of slow motion movie," Shin explained.[37] They made it through the entrance and received their asylum. After almost eight years of confinement, a simple right turn at an intersection had allowed them to regain their freedom.

Following their escape, Shin publicly explained that he and Choi had been kidnapped. Of course, Kim had a different story. The two had never been captives; they were guests in his country and absconded with stolen government funds intended for film-making. Their escape marked the downfall of the thriving North Korean film industry they had created. Soon their stirring films based on traditional national stories were replaced by the old propaganda work that had previously dominated North Korean cinema. Kim immediately withdrew all of Shin's films from international distribution. For years, *Pulgasari* would not be seen outside North Korea. Shin's name was removed from the credits.

Shin and Choi feared returning to South Korea. They worried that the authorities would never believe their bizarre tale and instead consider their actions indicative of a willful defection to the North, despite the fact that they had faced enormous personal risk in order to make secret tape recordings of conversations with Kim which exposed his disregard for his own suffering people. Their reluctance to return was also due to the burdensome censorship they had suffered as Shin's career in South Korea faded so many years ago. "I didn't want to come back to Korea right away because film censorship was too harsh. I didn't think I could make a film under the Korean government," Shin said.[38] So they lived in the United States for a while and did their best to avoid suspicion of communist sympathies. Shin was able to find directorial work under the name Simon Sheen.

Though Shin directed several films in the United States, his home was always South Korea, and that's where he and his wife finally returned. Shin had been through a lot. He had seen his career fade in the South, suffered years of imprisonment in the North, worked under the dictatorial command of Kim Jong Il, escaped the threat of death, lived in asylum and survived to see his home once again. Perhaps after all this he took solace in knowing with absolute certainty that it was his station in life to be a filmmaker. This was perhaps the only part of his life that remained consistent through all his difficult trials.

In his absence, the South Korean film industry and its audience had changed. Shin and Choi had grown older during their tumultuous years in North Korea, perhaps without noticing. The younger generations were not interested in the social ideology explored in *Mayumi* (1990) or *Vanished* (1994). But Shin endeavored to continue making the movies he wanted to make, despite the low box office returns. He still had plenty to say. "There are some movies that could never be made by young directors. I'm going to make those myself," he proclaimed, and he did just that until his death at the age of seventy-nine in 2006.[39]

In the twilight of his career, Shin finally had the chance to rewrite his past, or at least part of it. In 1996 he set out to remake *Pulgasari* as a new adventure called *Galgameth*. This time, the creature was benevolent and inspiring, and set out to help a young prince free his people. In one of his last films, Shin finally wrote the script that reflected his hopes for the world.

As of this writing, Kim Jong Il continues to rule North Korea and its film industry, which churns out approximately sixty films a year, all owned and tightly controlled by the state. The most visible artifact of Kim's influence on North Korean art is displayed on a sign outside the Ministry of Culture, which reads, "Make More Cartoons."[40] Of all the films he has produced, few exhibit a character as richly embellished and painstakingly developed as Kim himself. Prior to his death, Shin would eventually see the original *Pulgasari* reach an audience. In 1998 the film had its world debut in Tokyo and Osaka, Japan, the premiere date coinciding with the release of the American remake of *Godzilla*. Many believed Kim felt obligated to release the picture in an attempt to forge a new image of accessibility to North Korea. Others considered the decision to be a desperate effort to raise money amid a widespread famine. Though the theatrical release yielded little revenue, the movie now enjoys a cult following among monster movie aficionados.

Looking back on his life, Shin once noted, "With the tragic reality that not many veteran actors remain, I felt that someone needed to start achieving."[41] He did just that, and perhaps even more than he wanted to. "The highs and lows of life started to cross and I lived a path that was even more dramatic than the movies I directed."[42] The path was as unpredictable and uncharted as Kim's, and Shin was glad to leave that part of his life behind.

The dichotomy of Shin and Kim remains embedded in the flimsy celluloid of *Pulgasari* and *Galgameth*, two stories about creatures who possess enormous fortitude but exhibit it in different ways. In the end, both films live in obscurity. Shin's later movies, including *Galgameth*, reached only very small audiences. Even fewer have seen the movies he made in the North; Kim has kept a tight hold on distribution, and many of them have been banned.

Shin always wanted to reach the widest possible audience with his work, but ultimately, his own story is likely to be the most lasting, not the South Korean films or the big-budget *Pulgasari*. After all, they were only movies.

7

Black and Blue

The Crow

Ritual at Pentecost

ESTING IN THE VASTNESS of the Pacific Ocean is a small island called Pentecost, one of eighty-three islands that make up the nation of Vanuatu. However, there is something very distinct about the people who live there.

Twice a year, in April and May, following the yam harvest, the villagers perform a ritual called Naghol. It is a death-defying practice performed to ensure a successful harvest the following year, though in recent times it has also come to represent a rite of passage for the young male villagers. For the ritual, the boy ascends an eighty-foot-tall wooden tower onto a small platform. The people below provide song and dance, and the boy's mother, watching among them, may hold an item the boy cherished as a child.

With a vine tied to each ankle, the boy leaps from the platform headfirst. The vines will catch his fall just short of striking the ground. His head grazes the softened dirt, just barely touching, thus blessing the soil and ensuring its fertility for future harvests. The mother then tosses aside the boy's childhood toy, representing his successful passage into manhood. Other villagers will rush to the jumper and help him to his feet, removing the vines from his ankles. Then, another boy will begin his climb to the top, where he too will leap.

The event is so commonplace that men perform the feat repeatedly, sometimes for pleasure, sometimes in a show of additional support for the tradition, perhaps even to impress a woman. Deaths are rare, but not unheard of. One report claimed, "Before dives, it's common for men to settle disputes with family, friends, or wives—just in case they die."[1] One diver died during a visit from Queen Elizabeth.

Despite this risk, it seems curious that accidents are not more common. Behind the seemingly impetuous act, there is a great amount of attention paid to the details of the practice. The height of the diver must be precisely calculated. The moisture within the vine is measured to better gauge its elasticity. Too much give could be lethal; too little and the diver's head will not touch the ground and the soil will not be blessed. The arc of the tower must also be accounted for; if the wood bends too much when the vine becomes taut, the diver could be killed. There is an inherent danger in what these men are doing, but the goal is not human sacrifice; the goal is to live to see another harvest.

The simulation of death-defying acts—like those of the Pentecost villagers—is a Hollywood stock and trade. Often actors are put in risky situations where the unseen dangers must be carefully considered. Calculations must be made, details must be attended to, and standards must be followed. In the case of filmmaking, the pursuit is artistic, perhaps financial. For the divers, the pursuit is one of tradition. The villagers do not utilize any major technological innovations for the preparation of Naghol. But they are equipped with an understanding of what can go wrong when the rules of the ritual are not followed as tradition dictates. Just as the moisture of the vines, the give of the tower and the height of the diver must be considered, so too must the conventions of a Hollywood stunt, such as the chamber of a gun, the distance to an actor and the protocol of the illusion.

Eight Days to Go

"I get to play a rock-and-roll musician in it, and I get to play guitar and quote Edgar Allan Poe freely and come back from the dead."[2] This is how Brandon Lee described his lead role in his fourth feature film, *The Crow*. The film, a dark and mysterious story of the supernatural, was based on the 1989 comic book of the same name, written by James O'Barr and published by Caliber Comics. O'Barr made the book while he was coping with the death of his fiancée at the hands of a drunk driver shortly before their high school graduation. When asked in an interview, "How would you describe *The Crow*, the original idea, in one word?" O'Barr simply responded, "Bitter."[3]

On March 30, 1993, approximately fifty days into the shoot, the cast and crew were beginning to gear up for another night of filming. Only eight more days of shooting remained, after which most of the crew would return home. Brandon Lee, son of martial arts legend Bruce Lee, was on the cusp of completing his most critically and financially successful film. That night's scene would be shot on a sound stage at the now-defunct Carolco Studios in Wilmington, North Carolina. That night, they would shoot a complicated gunshot sequence in which Lee, as the character Eric Draven, would suffer the impact of a bullet to the chest. The prop master loaded the .44 magnum with a blank charge, a cartridge that has no tip but still contains enough gunpowder to provide the authentic flash and recoil of a real bullet.

In the scene, Lee would enter a loft apartment where two villains were assaulting a woman, and then Lee, with a grocery bag in hand, would be shot. A squib, a small explosive device connected to a blood packet, was rigged to provide the illusion of a bullet ripping through the grocery bag and into Eric's chest.

The weapons specialist had already finished his preparations and had left the set for the night. The prop master handed the gun to actor Michael Massee, playing the role of Funboy, who was to shoot the hero from a distance of approximately fifteen feet. The cameras began to roll.

Just as rehearsed, Lee entered the apartment, and Massee turned and fired his gun. The grocery bag exploded as the squib detonated, and Lee dropped to the ground. "It didn't really appear to the people on the set like anything was wrong," reported one eyewitness.[4] The scene continued as scripted, but soon it became clear that something was wrong; Lee was bleeding heavily from his abdomen. The actor was rushed to the hospital, where doctors discovered an entry wound approximately one inch in diameter. They conducted five hours of surgery to repair the substantial intestinal and vascular damage, but it did little to prevent internal hemorrhaging.

At approximately 1:30 p.m. on March 31, 1993, Brandon Lee was pronounced dead at the New Hanover Regional Medical Center in Wilmington. He was twenty-eight years old. His death provoked many questions and offered few answers.

Black and Blue

O'Barr's *The Crow* was a long time coming. Even before a drop of ink had hit the page, his tumultuous life shaped the tone of this dark tale. Raised in orphanages and foster homes, he passed through adolescence with many unexpressed emotions waiting to be absorbed by the pulp of a sketch pad. The dismal streets and abandoned buildings of his Detroit home presented a real life counterpart to the listless shadows of the comic book's urban battleground.

Around the time O'Barr first published *The Crow*, comics had returned to the public's consciousness with Tim Burton's film adaptation of *Batman*, which caused some early setbacks for his work. "The *Batman* movie caused me all kinds of trouble. All the printers were doing *Batman* material, and I couldn't even get black ink for my covers for a while. They had to use 'Midnight Blue.'"[5] Even the deepest blue couldn't approximate the darkness of these pages so saturated with despair.

O'Barr's path to success was fraught with false starts and tentative hopes. After several years of working on cars, he enrolled in medical school at the late age of thirty-two. The decision came after several failed attempts at selling *The Crow* to publishers. The deeply personal and cathartic project seemed destined to stay that way as O'Barr embarked on a new profession, though it wasn't long before the expense of his new education became a crippling burden, forcing him to drop out and return to automotive repair. It was at this impasse in his life when he finally caught a break; a comic book store owner offered to publish his work. Though initially a modest circulation, the book eventually sold 80,000 copies.

Never intended for a wide audience, *The Crow* was unabashed in its approach to violence. The fearlessness of writing only for himself may well have been the basis of the comic's success. "That's the best way to approach anything, don't write for an audience, but write for yourself so that way you're not setting up any boundaries. There are no hurdles you have to overcome when you write for yourself other than your own inabilities to get across what you are thinking or feeling," O'Barr said.[6] He remembered, "I was very self-destructive and the book was essentially one last love letter to this person. That was going to be it, the period on the end of the sentence. I had no idea what was going to happen to me after that. All the emotion is still there just creeping beneath the surface. It doesn't take much to put a scratch on it and let it bleed through. It's still a very personal work."[7]

The intensity behind the book struck a chord with many readers, and it was passed from one fan to another. Very little was spent on marketing its release, so the success of the comic was based almost entirely on word of mouth. One person to discover the work was the novelist John Shirley, who frequently delved into the darker realms in his own prose. One *New York Times* review noted, "Shirley's dramatis personae tend to be fairly unpleasant folks: killers, petty criminals, drug dealers, end-of-the-line substance abusers, Hollywood sleazeballs."[8] The description continued, "He writes about sensation unsensationally, with a particular tenderness toward those who manage, against the odds and by whatever means, to feel something."[9] While attempting to develop his own material in either the comic book or film medium, he discovered *The Crow* and found in O'Barr a kindred spirit.

Shirley, working with movie producer Jeff Most, contacted O'Barr while he was still completing the story. After lengthy discussions, Most was able to obtain a two-year option for the work. They agreed that O'Barr would still own the copyrights to the character and would be involved in all creative aspects of the film. The option was a ticking time bomb, a twenty-four-month race to find a studio interested in the project.

Shopping a film is a laborious task; the road to a contract is paved with rejections, punctuated with false starts and dead ends that can quickly consume the lifespan of the option agreement.

Jeff Most received over fifty rejections during the course of his two-year effort. The disinterest among studios was likely due to the perception that the material lacked marketability. Furthermore, the comic itself was still in its infancy. Toward the end of the option only two issues had been released, selling fewer than 2,000 copies. Traversing from one studio to another Most repeatedly weathered the rebuffs of dismissive studio executives like a pugilist entering the ring, round after punishing round.

Finally, Most made contact with the producer Edward Pressman. The eclecticism of Pressman's filmography indicated that he was not beholden to a single genre or style of film. Some of his previous works included *Das Boot*, *Conan the Barbarian* and *Wall Street*. There was no discernable thread passing through his list of productions other than maybe risk. But even Pressman required some coaxing. They offered him several revised drafts of the treatment, a written summary of the characters, plot and tone of the film. Pressman's reputation for ushering directors and producers into the dawn of their careers was an exciting prospect for O'Barr, Shirley and Most. He helped ignite the careers of Oliver Stone, Brian De Palma and Sylvester Stallone, and would bring more promising talent to the forefront with *The Crow*. The initial deal with Pressman only provided financing for writing the screenplay. The capital required for actually shooting the picture still had to be unearthed, though fashioning the comic into a script was an exciting first step.

Death by Misadventure

As Shirley began drafting the screenplay, a tension all too common in filmmaking started to mount. There were many different opinions about how to interpret the comic for film. John

Shirley had his own style, and he preferred staying close to the source material. His initial draft didn't coincide with the studio's interpretation, and after only the second draft, it was clear there was far more distance to cover between them than anticipated. Shirley recalled the orchestra of conflicting directives: "I was trying to respond to all these contradictory notes . . . trying to work in something for everybody according to the notes. And you know, I'd've done anything to stay on the project. They didn't give me the chance and I'm still bitter about it, frankly. I would've rewritten it a thousand ways to sundown and bled for it, but I did not get the opportunity."[10]

Ultimately, Shirley was fired, leaving him despondent. "I went into a deep depression for a while afterwards. I had to take antidepressants for like a year. I had a relapse. It was a drag."[11] Shirley would still receive a screen credit as a writer, but he had to share it with David Schow. Schow had experience writing horror and was at home with the dark material. Both writers made concessions, but the net result was a screenplay that represented a balance between light and dark. The final product certainly had sinister overtones, but a trace of vulnerability still penetrated through some of the characters. The next challenge was to find an actor who could embody both of these traits.

The talent for dynamic screen presence ran in the Lee family as much as the talent for martial arts. From the moment he was able to walk, Brandon Lee began training at his father's side. Bruce Lee was thirty-two years old and on the verge of international notoriety when he died on the set of *The Game of Death*, his fifth picture, in 1973. Brandon was just eight years old. There was a duality to Bruce Lee that he certainly passed on to his son. Beneath the taut muscle of the disciplined artist there was a surprising amount of levity. Bruce Lee loved to share little turns of phrase like "Seven hundred million Chinese can't be Wong."[12] While enjoying a lunch with a few journalists, he was served a bowl of soup and asked, "Now how in hell am I supposed to eat this with chopsticks?"[13]

Bruce Lee began to feel sick during a postproduction looping session for *Enter the Dragon* in May 1973. He excused himself to go to the bathroom and was found twenty minutes later, collapsed on the floor. He was sweating profusely and was struggling to breathe. They helped him up, but he collapsed again moments later. He was immediately taken to the hospital, where doctors discovered he was running a temperature of 105 degrees. He had an excess of fluid exerting pressure on his brain, indicating possible cerebral edema. Bruce managed to recover, though the doctors couldn't provide a satisfactory explanation for his condition. They could only reaffirm that Bruce was in remarkable physical condition.

The preliminary private screenings of *Enter the Dragon* were encouraging to Bruce Lee and studio executives alike. He was gaining momentum and ready to press forward, absorbing the stress and exhaustion of his burgeoning film career while developing his own unique martial arts style and also trying to be a good father and husband. But his recovery was short-lived, and on July 20, 1973, Bruce Lee died. Autopsies indicated the cause of death was linked to a severe reaction to an ingredient in the short-term pain treatment drug Equagesic. His death would be officially listed as "Death by Misadventure."

Upon learning of her son's death, Bruce's mother, Grace Lee, simply remarked, "Too much work."[14] Work had indeed consumed Bruce's life. *Enter the Dragon* was not the only film he was working on at the time of his death. He was a writer, director, choreographer and actor in *Game of Death*, which was still largely incomplete. It was a very personal project for him, but he had to set it aside when *Enter the Dragon* came along with a much larger budget. The raw, unedited footage of *Game of Death* was placed in a storage vault at Golden Harvest Studios. Years later, it was unearthed and an attempt was made to salvage the picture with the use of stunt doubles, extras and a small army of martial arts experts. The script had to be rewritten, and many liberties were taken in order to finish the film without the lead actor. In one scene, a cardboard cutout of Bruce Lee's face is used to simulate the actor's reflection in a mirror. The director's methods of completing the picture came under ethical scrutiny when he decided to use actual newsreel footage of Lee's funeral for a scene in which his character fakes his own death. Ultimately, only eleven minutes of footage from the original rushes were used for the film, which was released in 1978.

One Hundred and Twenty Percent

For Brandon Lee, *The Crow* was his first real opportunity to emerge from his father's legacy and into his own style. His earlier films had established his technical skills as a fighter, but *The Crow* would provide a more emotionally driven plot in which he might flourish as an actor as well.

In light of the many unfortunate events that would eventually befall the production, many claimed that the set, even the entire project, was cursed. The truth is far less mysterious; accidents are not at all uncommon on feature film productions. The intense action sequences of movies like *The Crow* frequently require the coordination of pyrotechnics, weapons, fight choreography and endless tangles of electrical wiring. But the first injury on the set came during a series of shots that didn't include any special effects. There were several scenes of Brandon's character roaming the streets at night. A crew member named James Martishius was several feet above the ground in the small cage of a mobile boom crane. After accidentally backing into a live power line, his coat caught fire. He suffered extensive second- and third-degree burns. The very same night, the interior of a grip truck was damaged when a blanket draped over the door ignited upon prolonged contact with a light bulb.

Complex logistics have exacted devastating tolls on stuntmen and crew members since the invention of film. Stunt pilot Paul Mantz died while completing an aerial maneuver for the 1965 release *Flight of the Phoenix*. Set dresser David Ritchie died during the production of *Jumper* when a portion of a wall made of frozen sand, water and dirt collapsed and crushed him. Stunt pilot Arthur Everett Scholl was killed while attempting a spiral maneuver for *Top Gun*. Harry L. O'Connor, the stunt double for Vin Diesel in the film *xXx*, was killed trying to rappel onto a submarine. In a more far-reaching tragedy, 91 members of the 220-person production of *The Conqueror* were diagnosed with cancer by the early 1980s. This has been attributed to the production location in Snow Canyon, Utah, which was downwind from the fallout of an extensive atomic bomb testing site in Yucca Flats, Nevada. The picture's producer, Howard Hughes, withdrew the film from circulation. In a less severe, though no less surprising incident, a bolt of lightning struck actor Jim Caviezel and assistant director Jan Michelini during the shooting of *The Passion of the Christ* outside Rome. "I'm about a hundred feet away from them when I glance over and see smoke coming out of Caviezel's ears," the producer Steve McEveety recalled.[15]

The tragedy that befell the production of *The Crow* sadly places the film within a category of pictures that has long existed.

However, in the early days of shooting, despite the first accident, the morale on the set was high, and many were impressed with Brandon Lee. The actor seemed to easily absorb the heavy physical demands of the shoot, which often left him covered in dirt, soaking wet, and working all hours of the night. He showed a rare combination of talent, selflessness, modesty and professionalism. The grandeur of the picture itself seemed to point toward a potential franchise for *The Crow* saga, which could launch Brandon's career into the stratosphere.

There is little indication that Brandon took any of this too seriously, though. Like his father, he took joy in laughing at the absurdity of not knowing what was around the next corner, and he took all the pitfalls in great stride. Lee used a portion of his salary from an earlier feature, *Legacy of Rage*, to purchase a 1959 Cadillac hearse. When a journalist asked him where he would like to end up, he responded, "Oh, in a little urn about this big."[16] Edward Pressman recalled that Brandon's goal was never to be a deeply serious or fierce person. Instead, "Brandon's dream was to be like Mel Gibson, goofy and charming and funny. But in quiet moments, when he thought about his father, he could be fatalistic."[17]

The work of feature film production is tedious and necessarily marked by difficulties and setbacks. Temperatures in the Wilmington location descended fast. "I've been colder on this film than I've been in years; I can never remember deliberately going outside when it was about 5 degrees, in the rain, with no shoes on," Brandon explained.[18] And O'Barr recalled, "They had to put alcohol in the rain machines to keep the liquid from freezing."[19] But some pictures, *The Crow* included, seem to persevere as a result of a unity among the cast and crew, and the nucleus of this bond must often come from the lead actor when the energies of the director won't suffice. Brandon, by all accounts, was very much instrumental in this capacity, and perhaps as much an asset to the production process as he was to the final film. One camera operator remembered, "He was there for it one hundred and ten percent, he really was. One hundred and twenty percent! The great thing is, with the difficult filming conditions—the rain and the cold, which makes it difficult—his attitude towards the crew always remained friendly and jovial." Jeff Most added, "Brandon was at home hanging out, talking to the production assistants or the craft service person who was carrying coffee. Brandon would join us at meals and it was always like the most uplifting spirit. When someone is giving of themselves in that manner, to everyone, it really creates camaraderie and a buoyancy for morale."[20]

After seven weeks of shooting and reshooting, production was beginning to wind down, and undoubtedly many were excited to return home. As the wrap became visible on the horizon, actress Sofia Shinas remembered chatting with Brandon. "I asked him what he was working on next. He said, 'Getting married.'"[21] Brandon was to marry Eliza Hutton just a few weeks later on April 17, 1993. Though he often expressed excitement for his wedding and tried to stay upbeat, the underlying truth was that the "conditions on the set had become subhuman," according to Jan McCormack, Brandon's manager who protested, "You guys are killing Brandon down there."[22]

March 31, 1993

There was a palpable pressure to complete the picture on schedule. Producer Jeff Most recalled, "We did cause concern to the bond company. That I remember. There was a bond company representative that we would see on location. I don't remember if he was physically there when the tragedy occurred, but I mean, we had run into concern because we were running through our contingency—the monies that are allowed, ten percent of your production budget, which are there for the purpose of allowing for poor weather, things falling behind, et cetera."[23] The presence of this person was an indicator that the progress and expenses of the picture were being closely monitored, and the people on the set likely felt that they had to continue filming without pause for any reason. But some of the shots that remained were among the most technically complicated and demanded extreme caution.

One of these upcoming shots required the use of dummy bullets. A real bullet is converted to a dummy bullet by removing the lead tip and explosive powder, then detonating the firing cap (the primer) at the base so that there is no explosion when the hammer of the gun strikes the bullet. The tip is then reattached to the bullet, giving the appearance of a live round. The dummy bullets were a necessary prop for a close-up shot of the revolving chamber of the .44 magnum. To present a convincing image, all six chambers of the gun would have to look as if they were loaded with real ammunition. This is where the lethal mistake would occur.

In addition to converting real bullets into dummies, the crew members were also converting them into blanks. A blank can be a dangerous device because it includes an explosive propellant. To make a blank, the explosive in the bullet is replaced with black powder to provide an authentic-looking flash when fired. The amount of force in the blank depends on how much black powder it contains; a blank can be designated as a "quarter-load," "half-load" or "full-load." The primer is left untouched so that the black powder ignites when the hammer of the gun strikes the flat base of the cartridge. Most important, the lead tip is replaced with wadding to hold the explosive contents of the bullet within the casing.

On that day, one of the blanks, mistaken for a dummy bullet, received a lead tip instead of the wadding that should have been used. As a result, one of the bullets loaded into the gun for the close-up shot was a blank with a lead tip and quarter-load propellant rather than a dummy. It would have been indistinguishable from the other bullets.

Veteran film and stage firearm safety coordinator Dave Brown explained the intricate science behind constructing the illusion of firepower:

> The terms '1/4,' '1/2' and 'full' load are essentially meaningless unless you are using them to compare the same manufacturer's loads in the same firearm. The power of a blank depends directly on how much gunpowder is in it and inversely on the square of the distance away from the muzzle. Also, all firearms have differing characteristics. Some have an open barrel, some use a restrictor plate and some have baffled barrels. There is no way to predict the hazard simply by the designation on the box. A 1/2 power .45 caliber blank can be more powerful than a full power 9mm blank. A 1/4 load shotgun blank is greater than a full power handgun blank, and rifle blanks can be 10 times more hazardous than the most powerful handgun blank.[24]

Clearly, all this involves a thoroughly intimidating array of calculations. Without keen attention to every conceivable detail, these blanks can be as dangerous as real bullets, especially when a tip is accidentally attached, as it was on the set of *The Crow*.

When the prop gun was first fired on set, the black powder provided enough force to discharge the tip of the blank, but at a lesser velocity than a real bullet. The force was not great enough for it to exit the barrel, and the tip became lodged within the firearm, where it remained unseen.

The cast and crew rehearsed Lee's death scene several times without the use of any rounds. A late change in the direction of the scene landed the gun in the hands of Michael Massee, playing Funboy. "I wasn't even supposed to be handling the gun in the scene, until we started shooting the scene and the director changed it," Massee remembered.[25] Earlier, when the blank was constructed for the scene, it was decided that it should be a full-load, providing the sound, flash and force of a real bullet. The force would also be great enough to propel the lodged lead tip out of the barrel at deadly speed. The director yelled, "Action!" and Lee entered the apartment. Massee pulled the trigger. The squib detonated, and Lee dropped to the floor just as rehearsed.

Initially, there was confusion about what had caused Lee's injury. "When that explosive charged, something from somewhere hit him," reported Wilmington Police Department officer Michael Overton.[26] "We don't know what that projectile was." At the hospital doctors performed several blood transfusions, reportedly using sixty pints, in order to replace the blood he was losing through an impacted artery. Cast and crew waited anxiously for updates. Police officers began their inspection of the set and the circumstances behind the stunt. Naturally, all possibilities had to be taken into account in their approach to discovering what went wrong. Early in the investigation, Police Chief Robert C. Wadman explained that they had not "crossed that threshold" of thinking that a crime was intentionally committed, though he remarked that the accident was, in fact, "suspicious."[27] Whatever precipitated the incident, the cause of injury soon became clear. "It's a bullet that killed him," remarked county medical examiner Leon Andrews.

Producer Jeff Most received a call in the early morning hours of March 31 and learned that Brandon had died. Members of the crew had already begun to piece together their theory concerning what may have happened. They slowly reconstructed the events of the shoot and the prior scene in which the gun was used. The lethal accident was caused by many crew members all making small mistakes. "Somebody really screwed up. Actually, a lot of somebodies screwed up. At some point, somebody has to take responsibility, at least in their own heart," fellow cast member Ernie Hudson said.[28]

After police reviewed the footage of the accident, they concluded that there was no malicious intent, so the tape was destroyed. Many in the press claimed that the misfortune was a result of a long-standing curse on the family. Of course, the real reason was less mystifying. "I don't think there was any doubt there was negligence on several occasions," remarked Wilmington district attorney Jerry Spivey.[29]

Any further decisions about the fate of the picture would have to wait. The director, Alex Proyas, returned home to Australia for a month, distraught and in mourning for his friend and coworker. He said, "Enough is enough" and refused to complete the picture.[30]

The Return

Brandon Lee was neither the first nor the last principal actor to die prior to the completion of a film. In 2008 Heath Ledger died before wrap on *The Imaginarium of Dr. Parnassus*. Director Terry Gilliam recruited Johnny Depp, Jude Law and Colin Farrell to complete Ledger's role in a variety of incarnations. Actor Bela Lugosi, cast in the low-budget *Plan 9 from Outer Space*, died before the first shot was filmed. The unrelenting director Ed Wood used salvaged footage of Lugosi from a previous project titled *Tomb of the Vampire*. In the remaining scenes, the actor brought on to replace him performed in a slouching stance and was partially veiled to conceal the fact that he looked nothing like Lugosi. The 1982 film *Trail of the Pink Panther* was also constructed without the presence of its lead actor, Peter Sellers. Unused outtake footage from earlier Pink Panther films, deleted scenes and various pieces of archive footage were stitched together in an unsuccessful attempt to make a cohesive picture. After Marilyn Monroe died in 1962, the film *Something's Got to Give* was confined to the darkness of a Hollywood vault. Only nine hours of the actress had been captured on film before it was shelved. The 1993 drama *Dark Blood* was left unfinished after River Phoenix's death, even though only eleven days of shooting remained.

Ultimately, Proyas changed his mind, and he and the rest of the cast and crew reassembled on May 26, 1993, to complete *The Crow*. "I don't think there was any doubt we could finish the movie at any time. Brandon had essentially finished his role. His part was essentially done," Pressman said.[31] For some the psychological fallout was devastating. "I just took a year off, and I went back to New York and didn't do anything. I didn't work," Massee admitted. "I don't think you ever get over something like that."[32]

District Attorney Jerry Spivey ultimately decided that the production company, Crowvision, and those associated with it would not be charged with negligent homicide. The announcement was a relief to many, but there was still an acute sense of loss among the cast and crew. This was an especially heavy burden during the month they would spend finishing the picture without Lee, literally pretending he was still with them. The financial aspect of the decision to complete the picture was also a factor, though CNA, the insurer of the film, "made it clear they would support us. The insurers trusted our judgment; they were not experienced in film production. They were supportive of what we were going through. And the truth is, if we didn't complete the movie, they stood to lose a lot more. Their risk will be reduced if the film is successful." The effort to complete Brandon's scenes sent the picture over their original budget of $15 million, though additional production expenses were not the only costs they faced. The North Carolina Occupational Safety and Health Administration fined Crowvision $84,000. Of this amount, $70,000 was for having live ammunition on the set. The remaining $14,000 broke down into two parts: $7,000 for the failure to properly check the gun before it was fired and $7,000 for aiming the gun directly at Lee. A subsequent appeal reduced the total to $55,000.

After extensive reviews and rewrites of the script, the team identified key portions of the plot that still required completion to make the story whole. They would have to reshoot Eric Draven's murder, the very performance that led to Lee's death. But one central problem remained: How could they complete the numerous scenes that required Lee? A variety of filmmaking techniques were employed to recreate Lee's presence in the film. Stuntman Chad Stahelski exhaustively studied footage of Lee's movements in order to faithfully recreate his walk and on-screen presence. They also used computer-generated imagery (CGI) where doubles would not suffice. This tedious process of "digital compositing" involved the painstaking task of removing Lee from each frame of one shot and placing him another. Additionally, voiceover narration was used to fill in gaps left by pieces of missing dialogue. Postproduction work added an additional $8 million to the original budget.

The complex visuals of the film had required extensive miniature sets to be constructed and shot with motion-control cameras. While the continuity, style and pace of the picture were all considered when producing these shots and making final cuts, the director and editor now also had to consider the implications of the violence. The film was already widely known to have claimed the life of the lead actor, and thus the gratuitous violence came to have uncomfortable connotations. "There was a real consciousness that we needed to enhance the emotional center of the movie as much as we could. We also eliminated little details—like images of Eric with bullet holes in his body. That was tough to watch, so we got rid of that," said Pressman.[33]

These edits, made out of consideration for Lee's family as well as his fans and everyone who worked with him, ultimately cost the film its distributor. In the terms of Paramount's negative pickup deal, they were no longer required to fulfill their contract because the film was now different from what they originally agreed to buy. In addition, the postproduction crew had been unable to meet the delivery schedule outlined early in the process. Paramount's executives publicly cited dissatisfaction with the amount of violence in the film as an explanation for its choice not to pick it up. This decision left many to speculate that the disturbing events surrounding Brandon Lee's death were the real motivation to abandon the picture, though the film was—and remains—a profoundly violent picture. Additional cuts were made after it received four NC-17 ratings from the Motion Picture Association of America.

Ultimately, Bob and Harvey Weinstein of Miramax took a chance and snapped up the film. It was released in May 1994, on

Friday the thirteenth, and made $11.5 million on opening weekend, a great success for the beleaguered production. Many reviewers extrapolated what may have been in Lee's future as a result of the film, had he lived. "Lee has a great presence, but who knows if this movie would have led to more mainstream parts for him? The truth is that the role of Draven didn't require a huge amount of acting," wrote one critic.[34] Another reporter claimed, "*The Crow* wouldn't have made Lee a top-dollar movie honcho, à la Arnold Schwarzenegger, had he lived. But it definitely would have given him a healthy nudge in that direction. He had the key attributes of a classic action hero—looks, voice, charm, athletic grace. All he lacked, it seems, was good karma."[35]

The film garnered immense profits from its theatrical and home video releases. The success of *The Crow* proved once again the Hollywood truism that there is always more story for a sequel. *The Crow: City of Angels* was released in 1996, followed by *The Crow: Salvation* in 2000. Neither of these two follow-ups approached the success of the original film. The story was later adapted into a twenty-two-episode television series called *The Crow: Stairway to Heaven*. Even this distant echo of the film was not free from the misfortune of the original production. In August 1998, a stuntman on the series named Marc Akerstream was struck on the head by a piece of debris from a staged explosion and died. The event was additional cannon fodder for those anxious to prove a long-standing "curse" on the production.

Newsweek reporters David Ansen and Mark Miller summarized the popular interpretation of *The Crow* when they wrote, "The movie leaves you with the excitement, and the sadness, of great potential lost."[36] O'Barr set out to come to terms with a personal loss and ended up creating a cathartic tale that reached an audience greater than he could have ever imagined. His art inspired more art, more comics, more films and more stories, but at an enormous price. The actor who brought O'Barr's work to the masses was gone, as was Brandon Lee's particular, irreplaceable interpretation of the character Eric Draven. In an interview conducted years after the theatrical release, O'Barr was asked if he believed in the afterlife. "No," he said. "It's a nice idea, but I just can't really seem to justify that in my head. I'd like to think I'm going to see Brandon again at some time, but in the real world, I don't think that's going to happen."[37]

Though the divers on the island of Pentecost cheat death and Hollywood actors are only meant to simulate cheating death, the goal remains the same: measure, succeed, survive. Somewhere in the process of filming *The Crow*, this crucial adherence to safety went by the wayside, communication broke down, and the protocol was abandoned. Measurements were not precise, calculations were imperfect, and details were forgotten.

8

Welcome to My Nightmare

The Abyss

The Postman's Palace

HIS HOME WOULD BECOME his life's work, requiring thirty-four years to complete. Measured in days: 9,000. Measured in hours: 65,000. Recounting how his building project began, Ferdinand Cheval, a postman in the south of France, wrote, "For the past three years I had reached this great equinox of life called the forties. This is no longer the age for wild enterprises and castles in the sky. It happened that just when my dream was gradually sinking in the midst of oblivion suddenly an incident brought it all back to me: I stumbled on a stone that nearly made me fall."[1]

The shape of the stone became the seed from which inspiration grew. The day after this first discovery, walking his usual mail route, he came to the same spot and discovered more stones, more unique shapes, more unique beauty. He gathered several of them, filling his mail pouch. The next day he gathered even more. Eventually he was unable to store his day's collection in pockets and pouches. He began carrying a basket on his nearly twenty-mile route and each day his acquisitions from the dusty ground were added to his pile. Soon the basket was traded for a wheelbarrow, and the insufficient hours of the day were traded for hours at night. "Then tongues started to wag in my home town and surrounding area. They quickly made their minds up: 'He is an old fool who fills his garden with stones.'"[2] These stones were to be the natural materials for Cheval's palace, an immense structure formed from an immense imagination. For now, only he could see it; others only saw the toil of a lonely man with a strange interest in rocks.

During his route, he imagined the arches, devised the spires, stacked the pillars and shaped the minarets of what was to be his castle, his vision. He dug the foundation in an empty plot of land, creating a base measuring eighty-five feet by forty-five feet. Without any previous knowledge of architecture or construction, the style of the structure would be as unique as Cheval himself, a blending of medieval chateaus, Arabian mosques, Swiss chalets and Hindu temples.

In time, he retired from his postman's position and devoted almost all of his time to building. After a lifetime of endless work, he finally moved into the sprawling palace with his wife. He was seventy-seven when his home was finally complete, and he was able to rest in the shade of his extraordinary creation. Its tall windows, twisting stairs and cavernous entrances are reminiscent of a child's sand castle. The eastern façade is made of animal sculptures and guarded by three giants towering over visitors with benevolent smiles. People from all over came to visit and see for themselves what Cheval described as the eighth wonder of the world.

The castle seemed absolutely magical to awestruck visitors, but Cheval knew the truth: "It is not a fairy tale but reality."[3] Tourists were amused by its free-spirited style, but Cheval knew that in every detail was a sore muscle. It was an expression of determination and work ethic as much as an expression of art. Only two years after finishing the construction of his own tomb on the site of the castle, Cheval died at the age of eighty-eight. He left the world to enjoy his work, a vast collection of stones slowly amassed and brought together to make his vision a reality.

Vision and inspiration are vital for successful directors like James Cameron. Like Cheval, his most trying project was initially something that only he could see. At first, Cameron knew little of the technical requirements of his project, just as Cheval knew little of masonry or architecture. Cheval did not rest until the palace was complete, and Cameron, too, refused to surrender until the last frame was shot. Though the process was perplexing to outsiders, both men knew they were embarking on a worthwhile journey.

Cameron's vision involved plumbing the murky depths of the ocean. It was not a project to be dashed off; it would take many tedious and laborious months to see the project through. Cheval's palace reached into the sky; Cameron's plunged into the abyss.

In the Great Wave of Gaffney

In the early days of August 1988, director James Cameron approached the crew for his latest picture, the underwater adventure *The Abyss*. Production was already behind schedule as they grappled with construction problems on the massive submerged sets. A brutal shoot consisting of twelve- to eighteen-hour days lay ahead. The monolithic scale of the tank—an unused nuclear reactor—where the most dangerous and complex shooting would be endured, was matched only by the imposing stature of Cameron's vision. Surveying the crew, Cameron simply said, "Welcome to my nightmare."[4]

"He's not the kind of guy who will say things in a diplomatic way. If you do something right, he'll say it was disastrous, but probably no human being could do it better, so you walk away thinking, 'I guess he likes it,'" Arnold Schwarzenegger explained.[5] The two worked together on *The Terminator*, a film that launched both of their careers in the early 1980s. At the time, Schwarzenegger was not yet a household name. As the years passed and the box office revenues grew, he reached the distinction of being among the highest paid actors in the world. Schwarzenegger's stardom did little to diminish Cameron's ferocity on the sets of their later films, *Terminator 2: Judgment Day* and *True Lies*. All orders were still to be followed, no matter how demanding or dictatorial.

It wasn't his fawning over Hollywood executives or the bravado of his high-concept scripts that fostered this style of leadership. Instead, like most leaders, his commanding manner was apparent at a young age. A combination of confidence and intense curiosity seemed to make filmmaking the most appropriate pursuit for young Cameron. It was in his youth that the first notions of his science fiction underwater adventure began. When he was seventeen, he wrote a short story inspired by a class field trip to a science lecture, where he first learned about underwater exploration.

Later, he became fascinated with the mysterious special effects methods behind futuristic films like *2001: A Space Odyssey*. He brought a scientific approach to realizing his stories that echoes from his days enrolled at Fullerton College. Cameron originally studied physics, a discipline that seems to have reinforced his interest in the mystery of the ocean. In an interview with *Omni* magazine, Cameron remarked, "Waves are fascinating, especially if you've studied physics. Once the energy has been expended to displace the wave, the wave can't be stopped."[6] His comment reads like a description of the enthusiasm for making *The Abyss*. He also hoped others would share his excitement. "I just assumed I could infect everyone around me with my enthusiasm. Like a tidal wave, what started as an incredibly ambitious project would reach a crest before sending all involved through a churning mess. People were going out of their way to tell me how crazy I was, but I kept telling them, 'Sure, it looks impossible on the surface, but we still have to do it.'"[7]

His lack of any formal film-school training presented no hindrance to his career, and perhaps even allowed him to develop a richer insight into filmmaking. "Film school screws you up. It takes years to recover. I think the basic requirement of directing is being able to anticipate what an audience wants to see. And having created something, what they want to see next." He continued, "If, at the age of fifteen, you immediately start becoming a filmmaker, you've lost that curative period where you're just a blank slate and you're reacting. I always remember in the back of my mind that if a movie plays at the drive-in, it's a good movie. And if the movie relies on the presentation being perfect, then it's a house of cards."[8]

Before he could convince any actors to join the project, Cameron first had to entice the studios. The enormous success of his 1986 release *Aliens*, a follow-up to Ridley Scott's *Alien*, made this task much easier. Cameron's science fiction thriller grossed $157 million worldwide with a budget of only $18 million. With revenues this strong, 20th Century Fox was just as interested in securing Cameron as he was in locking down the financing for his next project. Signing on with Cameron would also require a commitment to work with producer Gale Ann Hurd, whom Cameron married in 1985 during the development of *Aliens*. Fox executives were initially concerned about mixing personal and professional relationships, but their worries were soon dispelled by the widespread audience appeal of their collaborations. Cameron and Hurd proved they were a strong force, and the box office indicated this was a profitable relationship.

As he worked on other films, Cameron puzzled over the mechanics of his story for *The Abyss*, trying to reconcile his boyhood adventures with a cogent story about underwater exploration. The initially proposed budget of $50 million indicated that this sense of adventure had only grown with age. The project posed great difficulty, given the vast amount of underwater shooting that would be required. Many of the logistics for the most complicated scenes remained unresolved, perhaps not an uncommon predicament, but the scale of the story didn't help matters.

"*The Abyss* was really an all-or-nothing proposition," explained Gale Ann Hurd. "We either had to go with it right down the line or watch it collapse around us. We knew it was going to be tough going in, we just had no idea how tough."[9] Neither did the actors. On the page, the story was an entrancing and magical narrative, but it foretold little of the struggles that lay ahead. The script begins with the sinking of an American military submarine carrying Trident missiles. A team of navy SEALs is brought in to retrieve the missiles, working alongside a motley crew from an experimental deep-sea oil-drilling operation. Their operation has led to a startling discovery of a mysterious, luminescent, alien-like creature living in the depths of the ocean.

Many of the actors brought onto the project initially assumed that stunt divers would complete most of the challenging underwater scenes, though Cameron insisted that the rigors of the shoot were made clear from an early point. "I warned the actors, 'If you're claustrophobic, don't like water and are not prepared to work harder than you've ever worked in your life, don't take this part.'"[10] Any illusions the actors had about the comforts of a normal shoot were quickly dispelled when they began an intensive four-week diving class in Los Angeles. The course was designed to thoroughly acquaint the actors with the skills necessary to use underwater gear at depths of up to sixty feet. In order to allow the actor's performances to remain visible underwater, Cameron devised a special three-sided diving helmet that allowed the cameras to capture the actor's profiles. However, the greatest problem with the shoot remained finding adequate space to capture the action.

Filming in the ocean was not an option because of the corrosive properties of salt water. Existing underwater facilities were all inadequate for the scale of the picture. After exploring the idea of building their own underwater sound stage, it became clear that the costs would have quickly swallowed up far too much of the budget. In a short time, Cameron found himself with no real options and the project neared an early death. Then, in an uncharacteristically fortuitous event for the production, Cameron discovered a perfect solution in Gaffney, South Carolina. The Cherokee Nuclear Power Plant was originally constructed over a decade earlier and was never fully completed. The containment vessel was a large, cylindrical tank that could be filled with water. A smaller turbine pit could also be made into an underwater set, and both units could be converted into sound stages. To top it all off, it had recently been purchased by independent filmmaker and producer Earl Owensby.

The larger of the two tanks, A-Tank, could hold 7.5 million gallons of water; the smaller, 2.6 million gallons. The seemingly ideal solution presented its own unique set of challenges, one of which Cameron referred to as "tank weather." Prior to shooting, the crew installed heaters and filtration systems, but they couldn't completely eliminate the particulates that floated through the water as a result of the rust from the sets and sand at the bottom of the tank. Cameron summarized, "If you can only see forty feet on a 200-foot set, you're not getting your money's worth. We were always waiting for the water to clear or having to shoot something else. The shooting schedule depended on the tank weather."[11] The solution was to add substantial quantities of chlorine to the water, which led to its own problems, given the chemical's caustic properties. The performers emerged from the tank with bleached hair and chemical burns on the exterior material of their diving suits. Actors had to coat themselves in a thick layer of Vaseline to serve as a protective skin. Maintaining the clarity of millions of gallons of water became an imprecise science. Sometimes the water became so clear that the effect of the submerged environment was lost. The meticulous shooting schedule was at the mercy of this fluctuation between clarity and murkiness.

The relationship between Cameron and his wife Gale was equally murky during this time. Their three-and-a-half-year marriage was already largely behind them. Just prior to *The Abyss*, Gale had begun work on a film without Cameron: two people, two projects, two different sets of problems, and very few hours together. This fissure in their marriage widened amid the exposure of their difficulties by the press. "The script preceded any personal problems," Cameron explained. "The situation almost prevented me from making the film because of the scrutiny of my private life, which I protect. Then, I decided I could deal with it, as I am now. It wasn't a big enough disincentive to making the movie, which I wanted to do."[12] While writing the final draft for the picture, Cameron and Hurd were separated and headed for divorce.

The strained relationship between the two major characters, Bud and Lindsey, offers many parallels to the troubles between

Cameron and Hurd. "She's level-headed and scrupulous to a fault," Cameron said of his ex-wife.[13] In a Cameron film, anything can be put on the big screen, even the ensuing marital problems that lay ahead, perhaps unbeknownst to either of them. "This is an interesting coincidence of life imitating art, as the story predates our problems by about a year. Of course, a writer is always grappling with what's going on in his life while he's creating. Maybe I was prescient."[14]A complicated series of relationship problems in the script gave way to an unending sequence of production issues, just as their marital relationship became one of business— and a perilous one at that.

The initial euphoria among the cast of swimming and spinning around in the water during preliminary training faded quickly once the shoot started. On a regular basis, the actors were required to remain fifty-five feet below the surface of the water for three consecutive hours. The actors often waited on call for many hours at a time while a myriad of technical problems were solved. An early decision to begin filling both tanks even before the construction of the underwater set was complete was representative of the crew's constant race to outpace a flood of problems. They had to work day and night in order to build the underwater oil rig at a speed that kept them above the rising water.

The making of *The Abyss* reflected the artistry of problem solving as much as it did the artistry of storytelling. It was profoundly original in its ambitions, and thus much of the equipment needed to complete the shoot simply did not yet exist. In these instances, Cameron, along with his aeronautical engineer brother, Mike, collaborated to design their own underwater camera systems to provide more stable and smooth shots. Their work resulted in no less than five underwater camera patents. However, these improvisations were constantly being pursued by an ever-growing wake of problems.

Voltage

Before long, the reticence of the actors suffering under the demands of the production gave way. "I'm starting to have problems with the physical requirements of this movie," reported actor Ed Harris.[15] Many of these frustrations went unheard while they were beneath the water's surface; the communications system allowed Cameron to speak to the actors, but the actors were unable to speak to Cameron, "It was a director's dream, really," Cameron said.[16] Despite this one-way communication, underwater accidents were avoided through exhaustive preparation and the presence of a team of expert divers shadowing the actors. Each performer had an assistant just off camera, equipped to provide emergency relief. But the regular challenges of acting were still amplified by the constant unease of being in a close environment. Hurd remembered, "The biggest problem that we encountered early on . . . was that sense of being on the brink of panic. Relying on equipment which, as an actor, you normally don't have to do except as a prop and these were not props, these were life support."[17] The actors never felt a sense of genuine comfort with the equipment or circumstances. There was no reprieve from the physical and psychological discomfort of being confined to an underwater set.

Even those who were more familiar with these types of challenges were in awe of the scope of Cameron's endeavor. Underwater cameraman Chuck Nicklin said, "We did things on *The Abyss* that I didn't believe."[18] The painfully common twelve-hour days stretched on for twelve weeks; Nicklin spent much of this time locked within the stifling skin of his diving suit. His description of Cameron was a typical impression of those who have served in the director's platoon. "A lot of time we would be tired . . . but he would work harder than anybody," he said.[19] The extent of Cameron's hands-on approach cannot be overstated; by all accounts his efforts matched or exceeded those of the cast and crew.

For a director as galvanized as Cameron, it is no surprise to learn that the origins of his career began with a charge of electricity. In an early assignment to direct a pickup shot in the low-budget horror film *Galaxy of Terror* (1981), he was tasked with providing the effect of hundreds of teeming mealworms devouring a severed arm. After devising the setup for the shot, he was disappointed to find that the worms simply remained still. His solution was to run an electrical current through the artificial arm, jolting the worms into movement and creating a more dramatic scene. When he yelled, "Action!" an unseen assistant completed the circuit, causing the worms to writhe wildly. When he yelled, "Cut!" the assistant stopped the flow of electricity, and the worms returned to their motionless state. Two producers, casually strolling the set, saw what appeared to be Cameron successfully directing a horde of maggots to move and rest at his command. A short time later, he was offered the job to direct the feature *Piranha Two: The Spawning*.

The surge flowing through Cameron's projects has left many angry and disillusioned with the director and his intense demands. Novelist Orson Scott Card, who wrote the novelization of *The Abyss*, described the experience as "Hell on wheels."[20] He continued, "He was very nice to me, because I could afford to walk away. But he made everyone around him miserable, and his unkindness did nothing to improve the film in any way." Card concluded,

"Life is too short to collaborate with selfish, cruel people." However, Cameron has remained committed to his methods, asserting, "I shed not a single tear for the actors. Poor babies. It's the crew that's really busting their asses on the film."[21] But even the crew members were not free from Cameron's voltage. "Hiring you is like firing two good men," he was reported to have said to an employee.[22]

Cameron's acute attention to detail and his impatience for mistakes kept the actors safe on his films despite the potential for disaster. However, Ed Harris experienced a frightening event when a safety diver accidentally inserted a breathing regulator into the actor's mouth upside down, feeding him a mixture of air and water. Another safety diver spotted the problem and quickly assisted the actor. "It was a bitch, it was pretty hairy," recalled the actor. "The daily mental and physical strain was enormous."[23]

The discomfort of acting underwater was only exacerbated by the long hours. Cameron had designed an underwater filling station, which allowed the cast and crew to replenish their supply of oxygen without having to repeatedly resurface. While the challenge of keeping people in these working conditions was taxing, the problems with the underwater aliens were equally difficult. *The Abyss* was being made in the middle of a transitional period in the chronology of special effects development. CGI methods were just beginning to make an entrance in film production, leaving Cameron to rely on laborious practices of the past while simultaneously trying to develop new technologies. The script called for a translucent, bioluminescent underwater creature that swam and maneuvered like a real living entity. The complexity of building this alien allowed for very little testing or rehearsals, given the delicate nature of the designs.

Repeatedly, Cameron and the crew had to invent the solutions to their problems rather than scour an inventory of available resources. And, just as the technicians had to develop their own special audio and wiring systems, the cast had to develop their own ways of handling the physical and mental strain of long hours underwater. Harris remembered, "I don't think even Jim had any idea exactly how difficult [*The Abyss*] was going to be. There were a lot of unforeseen situations because we were doing things that had never been done before, so there was really no way of knowing what the difficulties were going to be until we were down there trying to do it."[24] Sometimes solutions came after careful preparation and exhaustive review of the problem. At other times the solution was simply the only remaining option. Such was the case when a hurricane destroyed the 200-foot tarp that covered the top of A-Tank. Sunlight shone through the surface of the water, thus ruining the illusion that the cast was thousands of feet deep. To maintain the darkness, Cameron simply shifted the shooting schedule entirely to nights, from 7:00 p.m. to 7:00 a.m. Later, a major pipe used to cycle filtered water into the tank burst. The repairs were just another bead on a string of unforeseen problems that mounted like the slow accumulation of water filling the tanks early in the production.

"We realized from the beginning that it was going to be difficult. What we didn't realize was that it was actually going to be impossible. Impossible in the sense that we never really got things under control. We were always in a position of being behind the eight ball," Hurd recalled.[25] The time and resources put toward solving a new problem meant that an equal amount of attention was subtracted from the normal protocol of shooting the film. These distractions from standard operating procedure reached a head one day during the filming of a pivotal and emotionally charged scene between the characters Bud and Lindsey. The scene depicted Bud bringing Lindsey back to life after being confined underwater without any breathing equipment. In the middle of the scene, the camera ran out of film and had to be reloaded. The cast and crew had already captured many usable takes, but Cameron wanted more. Mary Elizabeth Mastrantonio, the actress playing Lindsey, left the set in sheer frustration. She remarked, "Before it was over, I'd wanted to kill him at least a dozen times."[26]

Of Rats and Men

The Abyss earned Cameron a widespread reputation as a relentless taskmaster. "I'm letting you breathe. What more do you want?" he would offer to his actors in a tone that only slightly suggested sarcasm.[27] But the demands he placed on the cast, crew and himself were always equal, regardless of the size—or species —of the cast member.

During one scene, a character demonstrates an experimental method of breathing underwater using oxygenated water. A rat is submerged in the special fluid and struggles to escape before finally allowing the fluid into his lungs and breathing underwater. Cameron used no effects for this scene. He contacted Johannes Kylstra, a researcher at Duke University who provided the director with a detailed explanation of the steps and materials necessary to induce underwater breathing in the tiny cast member. The final step in the process required holding the rat upside down to allow the fluid to drain from the animal's lungs. After completing several shots of the scene there was suddenly a problem. The rat hung lifelessly. Cameron remembered, "I thought, 'Oh, shit, I'm not going to be able to get that little disclaimer at the end which says no animals were harmed in the making of this film, not with all these witnesses.'"[28] Quickly, he performed CPR on the rat and resuscitated him.

Cameron also came dangerously close to losing his own life during shooting. While directing underwater, he suddenly realized he was out of air—he couldn't breathe. The assistant director had failed to warn Cameron when his supply was down to one hour's worth. Cameron tried to communicate his situation to others over the PA microphone within his helmet, but there was no response. He made a horizontal slashing motion across his neck to signal his predicament to the support divers who normally hovered close, but no one noticed. Without any signs of help, Cameron disconnected his helmet, which was now nothing more than a thirty-two-pound anchor. He wrestled out of his buoyancy vest and began to swim to the surface while breathing out—a critical step to prevent his lungs from exploding during the rapid pressure change.

A safety diver finally noticed what was happening and stopped Cameron, forcing his backup breathing regulator into the director's mouth. Unbeknownst to the safety diver, the regulator was malfunctioning, feeding Cameron water instead of air. The diver struggled to keep Cameron with him underwater, thinking that the director was simply panicking. Cameron punched the diver, freeing himself from his grip, and finally made his way to the surface, gasping for air. Shortly after, he fired both the safety diver and the assistant director. With such a tight schedule, there was little question as to what would happen next: Cameron's helmet was retrieved and shooting continued. It was just another day on the set, though a particularly long one.

At the conclusion of a shooting day, Cameron would often spend an hour hanging upside down in the tank to acclimate to the changing pressure. While waiting, he arranged to have the dailies, the latest footage from the shoot, presented to him on a monitor through a plastic window. Cameron accrued approximately 350 hours within the square confines of his diving helmet. "Survival, pure survival" was the only way to deal with the challenges of the shoot, according to the director.

The collective efforts of the cast and crew were largely unknown to the studio executives who were thousands of miles away from the dark, murky waters of A-Tank. The schedule continued to slip, despite the long days and near constant work. As reports slowly drifted back to the Hollywood offices, executives ventured out to the set. After questioning the crew about the progress of the film, there was a confrontation with Cameron, during which the director let loose a string of shouted profanities. The unfavorable report that was sent back to the studio offices led to a 50 percent salary reduction for Cameron. The decision was well within the studio's power, given the initial agreement Cameron signed, which stipulated that such action could be taken to balance cost overages.

Many of these additional expenses were the result of the costly effects shots. Long after the actors departed, there were still several complicated special effects to shoot, all of which were critical to the storyline and impact of the film. In keeping with the cutting-edge practices of the production, the effects were achievable only through methods that had to be invented expressly for *The Abyss*. Even the decision to distribute the production of various effects among several different companies was a new practice at the time, which has since become a standard method for controlling costs and mitigating scheduling problems.

One particularly difficult effect consisted of approximately twenty shots totaling seventy-five seconds that would later come to exemplify the power of CGI as a tool in storytelling. The scene depicts a tentacle rising from a pool of water within the underwater oil rig, a benevolent attempt by the deep-sea creatures to contact the rig's human inhabitants. The effects team at Industrial Light & Magic was awarded the job of creating this signature effect. Their efforts for this brief scene would consume nine months, a span far too long to allow the director any time for a fallback plan. Their success was dependent on a major amplification of their digital resources and on the power of their computers. The simple resin sculptures that they started with would have to be realized digitally with all of the nuances and ripples of real water. Even the surrounding set in which the effect would occur had to be taken into account, given the reflective properties of water. Doug Kay, then CGI department manager at ILM, said, "Instead of just producing quiet little elements or wire removal and things you didn't see, the pseudopod was the key featured sequence, and it got great publicity."[29] The special effects work earned the team an Academy Award and was later used in the making of *Terminator 2: Judgment Day*. The effects work in *The Abyss* ushered in a new era of imaging. As Dennis Muren, a founder of ILM, explained, "The work on *The Abyss* was so astonishing because it offered a possibility of images that could be perfect."[30]

Resurfacing

As more shots were checked off the production list, their accomplishments began to shine through and the burden of making the picture diminished slightly each day. And so too did the water. As they finished all the large-scale scenes, shooting moved to a smaller C-Tank in Gaffney and to the Harbor Star Sound Stage in Long Beach, California. Next, they downsized to the 1932

Olympic swimming pool in Los Angeles for miniature shots, then down to Hurd's own pool. The final shot of the film, in which Mastrantonio and Harris reunite, was completed with two stand-ins on a puddle in a parking lot at Cal State.

The picture hit theaters on August 9, 1989. The box office receipts were less than what Cameron and the studios hoped for. After a final budget of $45 million, the film brought in domestic earnings of $54 million, a scant profit that was even more difficult to accept given the success of its theatrical competitors. "We came out the same week as *Uncle Buck* and made less money," Cameron said. "But who remembers *Uncle Buck* today? People are still watching *The Abyss*."[31] Despite Cameron's faith in his film, the majority of critics dismissed it as a confused story that failed to reach a cogent conclusion.

"Look, you run a marathon and, at some point, you snap the tape and you don't have to run anymore," Cameron explained in 1990. "I was running for eighteen months on *The Abyss*. The body has to catch up with the fact that you no longer have this great pressure. There is a great relief for me now."[32]

Film reviewer Desson Howe wrote in the *Washington Post*, "The Ending, as many moviegoers and other philosophers will refer disparagingly to the Industrial Light & Magic finale, is—like UFO sightings—best ignored."[33] Negative reviews and bad publicity came to dominate the discussion of the film even more than the narrative itself. But others still praised the inventiveness and ambition of the project, such as a writer in *Rolling Stone* who remarked, "Cameron may have fashioned his film out of familiar parts, but he's put them together in a way that demands fresh attention and respect. There's poetry in the images; *The Abyss* is pulp transcended. With probing intelligence and passionate feeling, Cameron has raised the adventure film very close to the level of art."[34]

For Cameron, the ultimate goal was to complete the film. Box office receipts and the praise of critics remained second to his ambition to see his story realized on the screen. "What it comes down to is that I simply couldn't not do it," the director remarked. But his achievement came at a cost. "I don't ever want to go through this again," he concluded.[35]

Eventually Cameron returned to terra firma and reunited with Schwarzenegger to make *Terminator 2: Judgment Day* and *True Lies*. He returned to the water in 1996 to explore the sunken wreckage that would be the inspiration for his next project, a love story called *Titanic*.

9

Rough
Waters

Waterworld

The Blockbuster Formula

THERE IS NO INVESTMENT like those made for film. The studio must make a commitment to the picture long before anyone can definitively say whether it's marketable or not. While sequels diminish risk, given a devoted audience, the studio is required to spend even more to appease so many with high expectations. Studios can perform test screenings to gauge the audience's reaction to a completed picture, though even this exercise comes after the money has been spent. There are no sure bets, only methods of minimizing risk.

One man who would become successful at the practice of minimizing risk was David Li. His world was not show business, but rather the equally unsteady terrain of the financial markets. Like other quantitative analysts working on Wall Street, he was, perhaps disparagingly, referred to as a "quant." In the late 1990s he began working for a consultant company called Risk Metrics Group launched by J.P. Morgan. He was tasked with developing his analytic skills into practical methods to be used in the financial market. Statisticians like Li don't delve into the glamorized world high-stakes traders and hedge fund managers enjoy. Instead, they work, often in solitude, through exhaustive calculations and equations to make sense of the unpredictable market. This unpredictability lives in the simple fact that incalculable connections exist between financial entities. Each has an influence on all others. If anyone could uncover how these connections work he or she would stand to yield enormous profits. Li began work on a formula that would do just that. His work came to focus on revealing the net of circuitry spread across numerous financial instruments.

Li eventually published a paper titled *On Default Correlation: A Copula Function Approach* in the *Journal of Fixed Income*. The article, spanning eleven pages, could be distilled to one short equation he developed that could be applied to the world of collateralized debt obligations. The purpose of the formula was to defray risk. His work showed how vastly complex risks could be simplified and thus more easily calculated. The result: The outcome of previously complex trades became more accurate. The equation unlocked trades that once represented too much risk. The formula was adopted by traders, rating agencies and regulators. The bond market exploded into a universe of profits and wealth. Li was referred to as "the world's most influential actuary."[1] Others began talking about Li's very real chances for a Nobel Prize. Meanwhile, trillions of dollars flooded into the market. It was the result of one man, one article and one equation praised for its truth and simplicity.

Then, something unexpected happened; the formula faltered. Investors failed to understand that it was possible for a large number of people to default on their homes at once and that, in fact, one default could beget another. Li himself offered, "It's not the perfect model."[2] Billions were lost. The result was the collapse of the U.S. subprime housing market. An infamous

Rough Waters

lesson was learned once again; no predictive formula is perfect.

If such a formula could have been used by studio executives it surely would have been. But their only equation rested on the dubious truism that a combination of big stars, big action, high-concept scripts and massive special effects results in profits. Like Li's equation, this big-budget summer-event-picture model had been used to great success in the past and continued to pay off for numerous studios. That is why so many became enraptured with a little-known script titled *Waterworld*. It had all the elements that were so important to financially successful films. However, once again, the formula showed its own fallibility. Just as so many traders invested their faith and capital into the efficacy of Li's model, the studios invested similar wealth into the notion that any visual thrill would draw a crowd and profits.

Hollywood's confidence in its formula seems justified. American audiences had long ago established an appetite for big-budget event pictures and even the theaters were happy to feed this hunger. Not only had the average motion picture budget reached $35 million, but some of the more successful releases consumed $65 million in costs. Movie theaters expanded their presence by more than 30 percent from 1993 to 1998 with a jump of 28,000 movie theaters to 37,000.[3]

The formula worked before and it was believed that it would work again, until it began to show its shortcomings and inconsistency. The mounting costs of *Waterworld* indicated not only a production out of control, but also a strong allegiance to the blockbuster formula. As the stakes increased, more cash was invested in the belief that future revenues would overshadow the expenses.

Long before the completed movie reached theaters, some involved in the picture became quietly (others not so quietly) doubtful of this model. In the meantime, the true fate of the film remained uncertain. Money continued to flow into other big-budget features in production. Jason E. Squire, former feature film executive for 20th Century Fox, writing in the early 1990s, explains, "By 1990 high-risk, high reward picture-making was supposedly warranted in light of the potential global return from theatrical, home video and other formats." He continues, "The mainstream studio product, whose mass audience expects 'tent-poles' of entertainment during summer and winter holidays, con-tinues to escalate in cost, making the stakes higher than they have ever been."[4] The diversification of pictures shrank as larger bets were placed on fewer movies.

Throughout its production, *Waterworld* slowly eroded the faith of more and more in the blockbuster formula. The picture was far past the point of no return, leaving everyone looking to the outcome as the final indicator of whether this formula was valid or not.

Rough Waters

The largest picture ever produced in its day started with the humble beginnings and aspirations of a young college grad named Peter Rader. After graduating from Harvard, he made his way out west to Hollywood in 1983, where he entered the low ranks of menial production jobs almost completely occupied by others working to engineer their own success in the film industry. While the big production of *Waterworld* lay in his future, his best chance at real opportunity in his early days would come from the low-budget realm, and in this arena one man reigned king, Roger Corman. Though the pictures at his production company New Horizons were decidedly of the B movie stature, many of those involved went on to become some of the most influential names in the business. James Cameron, Ron Howard, Martin Scorsese and Francis Ford Coppola all participated in pictures produced under Corman.

Rader struck up a friendship with Brad Krevoy, a close associate of Corman's. Krevoy indicated that if Rader could put together an adventure story, he stood a real chance at seeing his picture come to life at New Horizons. Rader remembers, "He told me that if I would write a Mad Max rip-off, he would arrange financing and I could have a hand at directing. I went home and thought about it and decided that I didn't want to do another Mad Max rip-off. It seemed like everyone was doing them—it was the classic low budget thing to do. I wondered, 'What if we set the whole thing on water? I went back and pitched it to him and he took one look at me and said, 'Are you out of your mind? It would cost us three million dollars to make that movie.'"[5] A small-budget film would normally require just a fraction of this amount.

This initial setback emboldened Rader to write a script that met his vision without having to work within the confines of a small budget. Whether or not he believed the script would ever reach an audience, it seems clear the definitive no from Corman meant he could let the picture bloom in full color in his mind and on the page, even if that's where it would remain. Rader explains, "I thought about what I wanted to see on the screen."[6] Using a computer borrowed from his cousin, he drafted the script. This same cousin, working as a line producer, offered to share the script with Lawrence Gordon, who had produced several successful pictures and would go on to produce blockbusters like *Die Hard* and *Field of Dreams*. Rader, citing shyness, declined his cousin's offer and subsequently shelved the script for three years, believing it had little chance of success.

In the intervening years, Rader became closely acquainted with, and eventually disillusioned by, the B movie genre pictures on which he worked. His career, though, had left him with many industry contacts, so he took another look at his unproduced script. "I dusted off my *Waterworld* script and I thought, 'You know, this isn't bad. It's actually kind of good.'"[7] After a rewrite Rader shared the material with producers Andy Licht and Jeff Mueller (*License to Drive, Little Monsters*) who loved it and helped Rader find an agent. The script then, quite ironically, found its way to Lawrence Gordon who shared the others' enthusiasm for the project despite Rader's hesitation years earlier. A deal was signed on Christmas Eve of 1989, earning Rader $350,000 for the script and an additional $150,000 if the picture reached completion. However, the heavy budget required for production necessitated a relationship with a big studio. Universal finally signed on to the project in 1992, and development kicked into high gear.

A search for various directors to helm the pictured finally became focused when Kevin Reynolds expressed interest. He was a welcome addition to the project, given his recent success directing *Robin Hood: Prince of Thieves*, costing $50 million and bringing in $390 million in worldwide distribution. Given his working relationship with Kevin Costner on the adventure tale, as well as the earlier picture *Fandango*, it seemed joining the two for *Waterworld* was an obvious next step; however, Reynolds initially advised against including Costner. Despite the success of their collaborations, their relationship remained strained after numerous creative differences and logistical problems experienced on the set of *Robin Hood*. In an effort to settle these past differences, Lawrence Gordon arranged for Reynolds and Costner to meet in Lake Tahoe during shooting for *The Bodyguard*. The two reached a middle ground and restored their relationship—or as Costner later remarked, "I thought we did."[8]

Their relationship devolved once again after *Rapa Nui*, a 1994 release and personal project of Reynolds's who wrote and directed the picture with Costner acting as a producer. The movie failed in the box office, earning $305,000 domestically on a budget of $20 million. However, this setback, like so many others that lay ahead, would not derail *Waterworld*. By this time, the project, beginning in June 1994, had already spent nearly half its budget of $65 million. A total of $30 million had been paid to talent like Costner (claiming a reported $14 million salary) as well as to the director, other actors and writers who had been brought in to revise the script above the already seven revisions Rader completed. Jeanne Tripplehorn joined the cast as the lead character's love interest. Young actress Tina Majorino, only ten years old at the time, won the role of the adopted child holding the key to dry land. Her auditions were successful to edge out the other front-running contender, Anna Paquin. Dennis Hopper was later cast as the chief villain.

The shooting script came to take on a very different look than the original, which featured a hero named Noah, who traveled the sea on a river barge, keeping a white stallion as his only companion. The backstory indicated a nuclear holocaust as the reason for decimated polar ice caps. It was later decided that the disaster precipitating the drenched Earth in the story would be the result of global warming. Constant narrative changes such as these, came to consume valuable time and money needed for the production. The start to principal photography approached, while new writers were tasked with rewrites including Joss Whedon (*Toy Story, Buffy the Vampire Slayer*) who remarked, "I refer to myself as the world's highest paid stenographer."[9] He continues,

"Waterworld was a good idea, and the script was the classic, 'They have a good idea, then they write a generic script and don't really care about the idea.' When I was brought in, there was no water in the last 40 pages of the script." Whedon elaborates on the process saying, "I was there basically taking notes from Costner, who was very nice, fine to work with, but he was not a writer. And he had written a bunch of stuff that they wouldn't let their staff touch. So I was supposed to be there for a week, and I was there for seven weeks, and I accomplished nothing. I wrote a few puns, and a few scenes that I can't even sit through because they came out so bad." Whedon received no credit for his additions to the film. He remarked, "By the way, I'm very bitter, is that okay?"

The writers invited to the project seem to fall into two distinct camps: those who worked to serve Costner, and those who worked to serve the story. One of the original intentions behind the movie was to match the originality of the concept to an equally original action hero that would become the face of a more complex, character-driven action genre for the '90s. The disagreements concerning the script continued as production drew closer.

While the abstract issues regarding the characters were ironed out, others attached to the film, like production designer Dennis Gassner, were tasked with more logistical concerns like finding a location for the shoot. After twenty-four days and eighteen flights spent scouting regions in Australia, New Zealand, Malta and the Bahamas, he finally settled on Kawaihae Harbor on the island of Hawaii. The location offered the ease of flights to and from Los Angeles. Gassner's find also offered turbulent seas, evident not only during the tumultuous shoot, but also in the very name of the location itself which means "rough waters." The location also featured a large warehouse-like structure once part of a sugar mill that could be converted into a studio for interior sets. Once again, this seemingly fortuitous circumstance presented a liability; the local economy had faltered after the closing of the mill, and those who could provide services to the production, such as supplying steel and portable restrooms, knew they were the only locally available option and charged accordingly. Those who were not suppliers would offer themselves as a resource for casting agents who were looking for 300 extras.

Enormous expense and time was also devoted to the task of designing the hero's boat—a sixty-foot trimaran featuring a central hull flanked by two other outrigger hulls. The craft would have to be constructed in such a way as to allow Costner to perform as if he was controlling the boat while, in fact, the vessel would be controlled by others. As a result, the boat would have to be manned from inside the hull, a logistical problem requiring painstaking preparation. Jeanneau, a French boat company, offered a similar trimaran that could be fitted with the counterweights and esoteric gears necessary to give the hero's craft a weathered, retrofitted look that could pass as a makeshift boat on the waters of a distant world in the year 2500. The production required two boats though, one for shoots showing it sailing in the open sea. The other was a more complicated ship designed to transform from trawling to sailing mode when confronted with danger. Constructing such a complex structure involved a team of engineers working with various gears and heat-curved, high-grade epoxy fiberglass. The total expense of the construction came to a reported cost of $500,000 for each boat.

The planning behind erecting the two trimarans was second only to the primary set piece of the film referred to as "the atoll." This sprawling structure represented the quintessential visual to boost the film's production value and in time would consume far greater expenses than planned. Initial discussions focused on the idea of shooting the piece in miniature; however, this concept was abandoned early in the planning. Gassner explains, "There was live action in too many situations for us to have done this as a miniature." He also confesses, "It was something I'd never done before—it was something nobody had ever done before. And we had one other important consideration: time. We knew that if we wanted to shoot by a certain date, plans for the atoll needed to begin immediately."[10] The structure had to be convincing on screen as well as sturdy enough to withstand the open sea and the burden of a lengthy shoot consisting of numerous action sequences. The final product was designed to span a quarter of a mile in circumference.

Split into eight separate sections, the atoll's pieces were brought together to form a ring-shaped fortress. Each of these pieces needed to float, and after extensive research it was determined that several large steel barges made of hollow tubes anchored together with I beams could serve as a floating grid, or foundation upon which the set would sit. While this solution seemed to solve the problem, it only revealed another; just who could assemble such a base for the set? The magnitude and complexity of such a design was very much outside the realm of even the most seasoned motion picture set builders. Ultimately, the job was given to the company Navitech, a subsidiary of Lockheed, located in Honolulu. The raw materials alone presented dizzying expense, as the atoll required over 1,000 tons of steel. The final set, designed to resemble a desperate shelter, represented a whopping $5 million expense on the books of the production. The location of Kawaihae delivered on its reputation of turbulent waters, making another set unstable and eventually causing it to sink.

The scale of the picture and daily setbacks became too large to conceal, and it wasn't long before the media found that they had a story. It was the beginning of a long series of articles and television spots that came to characterize the film in a much more negative way than any of the studio promotions could combat. Even *Time* magazine acknowledged the media frenzy when a staff writer remarked, "The location nightmare of Universal Pictures' adventure movie has been assiduously chronicled: how the *Waterworld* shoot in Hawaii was threatened by crew injuries and tsunami warnings; how a huge set sank toward the end of shooting; how the budget ballooned from $100 million to what now may be twice that; how the star, Kevin Costner, and the director, Kevin Reynolds, fought over various aspects of the film until Reynolds stormed out during the editing. Things can go wrong in movies; it's part of the gamble. On *Waterworld*, everything went wrong."[11] While some journalists delighted in the failures of the production other writers took notice of the effect of this unfavorable press.

It's evident that the negative news about the production would always find a greater readership than reports of any success, as few as they might be. Costner, much like the director, had to shoulder some of this burden, as he, along with the special effects and action, would need to carry an even heavier film now that the press had started to attack. Later in his career, Costner wondered about this environment of schadenfreude: "The press says it will be a disaster. I don't quite understand this climate of hostility. Why doesn't everyone pull for the picture? I try to make the best picture I possibly can each time out, but I made it my way. That's the only way I can make it."[12]

Oscar Wilde has said, "The only thing worse than being talked about is not being talked about," and that seems true of *Waterworld*. As unwelcome as the negative reports were, they had the effect of increasing awareness of the film and inviting viewers to have a reason to join the fray by watching the movie. On the quaking waters of the set, this truism was scarcely felt and only added to the pervasive concern of a picture spiraling desperately out of control. It was reported that Dennis Hopper offered to share a tabloid headline with Costner who only offered, "I don't ask for a lot on the set," he says. "Be quiet, don't read my tabloid headlines to me."[13]

Kevin's Gate

While Costner and Reynolds endured their relationship with each other, the other cast members began to feel the stress of a shoot that threatened to extend well past the unrealistic schedule of ninety-six days. Jeanne Tripplehorn, in 2009, remembered, "In retrospect, I realize it made me reluctant about films. There were things that were so out of my control and a bit overwhelming."[14]

The complex choreography of the film's action gives no indication of the stagnant pauses that plagued the production. For reasons of verisimilitude, the cinematographer and set crew struggled to ensure each shot avoided any indication of land in the distance. Any interruption to the vast water of the story would require expensive computer-generated work in postproduction. This mid-'90s digital work was painstaking and expensive and often used sparingly. For this reason, many were amused to read the apocryphal report that Costner demanded his hairline be digitally improved. The star's response? "Bullshit."[15]

Meanwhile, those literally behind the scenes became frustrated with the project. Fierce winds and jostling sets threatened the safety of countless extras, often requiring care from on-set medics. Jellyfish stings were common, and a far more serious embolism nearly took the life of a stunt double who was rushed to a Honolulu hospital. The distance of this trip was taxing, as evidenced by the nearly 200-mile journey endured during the delivery of the atoll set, shipped on barges, from Honolulu to Kawaihae. Each of the eight pieces required careful placement into the water. The crew responsible for the atoll set in Hawaii reached as many as 500 workers. It seemed no craft or set piece was without its own unique set of challenges. The villain's vessel, a 1,000-foot supertanker, was another problem. Obtaining and shooting on a real tanker was out of the question, given safety concerns and budget. Instead, plans were devised to build a 550-foot deck serving as the tanker, which used the technique of forced perspective to achieve the illusion of a ship nearly twice that size. These difficult structures consumed a year and a half of preparation before even one scene was shot. With such enormous investments, the shoot needed every bit of good fortune it could afford. As a result, the local shaman was brought to the set to initiate a ceremonial blessing viewed by the cast and crew, eager to see the picture become a success.

The numbers began to illustrate a different fate for *Waterworld*. The already unrealistic budget had long since dissipated as costs climbed, placing greater stress on the picture. Some began to see the even greater impending problems and jumped ship. Designer Peter Chesney and effects artist Kate Steinberg left the project, followed by the the first assistant director. While Costner remained surrounded by an army of extras and cast members, the conspicuous exit of these teammates likely took a psychological effect. Morale was shaken as others undoubtedly questioned whether it was their time to go. Now an international star, Costner was accustomed to a plethora of assistants and rainmakers eager to please, but this setback perhaps momentarily reacquainted him with the early days of his career. The continuation of his well-established hit streak came into question for the first time.

The struggles experienced on the picture seem at odds with history. The familiar aspects of American romanticism that permeated Costner's other successful projects were also present in *Waterworld*. Why then would the outcome of *Waterworld* be any different? The rampant rumors about egos on the set seemed to discourage the love affair so many movie fans had with Costner's typical strong-and-silent-type character. The public consciousness had been influenced by what they had seen in films like *Field of Dreams* and *Bull Durham*, and now it seemed the media was portraying a real-life Costner who was far less likable. Noticing these unpleasant reports, MCA president Sid Sheinberg explained, "If you're looking for a villain, it's not Kevin Costner, it's the calendar."[16] From the beginning the schedule was unrealistic.

It seems there are two Costners that have come to exist in the perceptions of his fans. There are those who see him as the embodiment of all his likable characters, and those who have come to view him through the articles and quotes pertaining to his command of the set. When the productions and pictures are a success, the persona of a star like Costner can be controlled via planned anecdotes and sound bites. When things fall apart, these scripted talk show appearances come to serve another purpose; he must defend the picture and decisions.

Tabloid stories began circulating weekly on the problems with *Waterworld*, or what some called "Kevin's Gate." Reports of frivolous spending added to the bad press. Details on expenses, like those written years later by James Robert Parish, indicated "the star's land accommodations at $1,800 a night, the $800,000 yacht acquired to ferry Costner from the island to the set some 400 yards from shore." He goes on to list other costs that could have been avoided, including "the $2.7 million lost to union penalties for the staff food breaks that were nearly always late."[17] While this bad press represented a threat to anticipated ticket sales, the more immediate concerns of cost had to be handled.

These escalating costs, now shouldered in part by Costner, did not necessarily translate into greater images on screen. In fact, much of the spending went toward resources, such as the one hundred water safety crew members consisting of off-duty fire-fighters, rescue divers and lifeguards. A small medical clinic was established fifteen minutes from the set. Other crews were tasked with constantly monitoring the surrounding water to remove any debris that might break loose from the set. Additional funds were spent to procure the countless pieces of set dressing for the atoll. All of these artifacts had to be aged to provide the look of junk that had been retrieved from the surface hundreds of years after the deluge. This meant filling eleven forty-foot-long shipping contain-ers with discarded junk from Hollywood prop houses. All this material required two weeks to complete the journey from Long Beach to Kawaihae. One such container held seven and a half tons of cotton netting also to be used in dressing the set. The monochromatic design of the sprawling set was appropriate for the realistic look of the production. However, all of these painstak-ing details were often lost amid the fast cuts and blending colors of the shoot. Additionally, the costumes, also the same color palate as the set, blended into the atoll, making many of the cast mem-bers difficult to see. Apart from these additions to the set, some have estimated the individual props in the film reaching approx-imately 10,000 pieces, including spears, arrows, machine guns and handguns. These problems were all minimal, however, compared to the difficult logistics required for constantly rotating the atoll so that all the shots required for the day would show nothing but a vast sea in the distance. One rotation consumed six hours, completed in the darkness of night so as not to interrupt daytime shooting.

The daylight shoots provided even greater challenges, such as the evil Smokers' attack on the atoll, which occupied four days of continuous action shots. The sequence required twenty-eight Jet Skis, each modified to make the internal exhaust systems external in an attempt to fit the look of the film. Gunboats were built from World War II–era hardware capable of firing waterproof blanks. "On a heavy effects day we averaged about 3,000 bullet-hit effects, that meant 3,000 squibs, zirc balls, sparking granule balls, and dust capsules. It wasn't unusual to have between six and eight guys with guns shooting continuously," noted effects supervisor Marty Bresin. One shot alone consisted of 1,200 bullet hit effects, each blowing an eight-inch hole in the side of the atoll. The entire barrage spanned 300 feet. The scale of the picture required the professionalism of 154 special effects technicians, a record at the time. The ultimate accomplishment of their planning can be seen in a climactic ending scene involving the villain's barge. The stunning sequence involved twenty-five fifty-five-gallon barrels which were launched into the air. Additionally, the effects team spent 700 gallons of gasoline to provide the realistic look of an oil tanker igniting. Safety became a primary concern, and as a result, each action sequence was carefully rehearsed and rerehearsed. The preparation of each shot took hours starting with the coordination of countless extras, each wearing his or her own unique costume picked from a stock of 2,000 sea-inspired pants and jackets.

These live action stunts and pyrotechnics were used in conjunction with equally complicated visual-effect shots reportedly numbering 350 in total. Some of these shots required extensive underwater photography, for which special camera housing was designed. Communication between the director above water and cast and crew below was achieved using an underwater PA system and water-to-surface video playback. All of this communication could only be achieved when the forces of nature allowed. At times a warning siren would sound indicating that everyone was required to take cover due to weather.

The toll on the cast continued, and director Kevin Reynolds was beginning to feel the cracks. He later remarked on the film-making process that "about 50 percent of directing," he laments, "is about subjecting yourself to the process."[18] His days directing *Waterworld* were a distant reality from the predictable nine-to-five world he left years ago. He once recalled the fortuitous turn of events that ignited his career. It all started with a short student film he wrote and directed called *Proof.* Spielberg, already a household name, saw the film and was impressed. Shortly after, Reynolds received a call: "He asked me what I wanted to do, and the next day his production assistant calls and says, 'Steven is making arrangements for you to make an expanded version of *Proof*,' I hung up and sat in a chair for about an hour. Then I called her back and asked, 'Could you please repeat everything you just said?'"[19] It was the beginning of his career; he was only thirty years old. The exuberance of this victory became tempered over time, and his discussion of *Waterworld* years later can be read as a history of the production or a deeper musing on the entropy of life. Reynolds explains, "But when you're on water, everything's constantly moving apart, drifting apart, so you have to try to hold things down somewhat."[20] It is true not only of the shoot, but also of all aspects of the film. His relationship with Costner drifted; his control on the film also came loose.

There are some things Reynolds and Costner did agree on; they both have noted the delight the press took in reports of difficulties on the set. Both identified the simple fact that bad news read better than good news. Reynolds recalls:

> People wanted to have bad press. That was more exciting to them than the good news. I guess the most egregious example of that that I recall was that the publicist told me that one day, we'd been out the day before and we were doing a shot where we sent two cameras up on a mast of the trimaran and we wanted to do a shot where they tilled down from the horizon down to the deck below. We're out there, we're anchored, we're setting the shot up and a swell comes in, and I look over and the mast is sort of bending. And I turned to the boatmaster and I said, "Bruno, is this safe?" And he looks up the mast and he goes, "No." So I said, "Okay, well, we have to get out as I can't have two guys fall off from 40 feet up." So, we had to break out of the set-up, and go back and shoot something else and we lost another half-day. Anyway, the next day the publicist is sitting in his office and he gets this call from some journalist in the States and he goes, "Okay. Don't lie to me—I've had this confirmed from two different people. I want the facts, and I want to hear about the accident yesterday, we had two cameramen fall off the mast and were killed." And, he goes, "What are you talking about?" And he [the journalist] goes, "Don't lie to me, don't cover this up, we know this has happened." It didn't happen! People were so hungry for bad news because it was much more exciting.[21]

The event was one of an incalculable number of manufactured stories. The frequently cited story of the atoll set sinking was based in the much less dramatic fact that it was actually a much smaller, separate set that sank. Could the bad press be quantified in dollars? Reynolds has indicated that a previous MCA head believes the negative press cost $50 million in lost ticket sales.

As shooting dragged on well beyond the schedule, actors grew tired and often became additional set pieces to a picture where the action and effects took the lead role. Dennis Hopper was weary and had little to say, only offering that his roles of late such as those in *Waterworld* and *Speed* offered little in the way of latitude when it came to developing the character. Speaking to interviewer Charlie Rose, he commented on his memorable mid-'90s psychopath Howard Payne in *Speed*, "My character's just there to push the action on." He felt a lost opportunity for "the great role I don't feel I've ever really had."[22] *Waterworld* would not bring that opportunity. The young Tina Majorino was treated for repeated jellyfish stings. Tripplehorn also struggled, noting, "I was feeling a little like Patty Hearst. I was just completely brainwashed by my captors and I was just out there trying to get through it."[23]

With so much financially invested the picture, there was no option but to continue the shoot with hopes for a successful summer release. The original schedule calling for ninety-six days of shooting had long been forgotten as the cast and crew drifted past 100 days, then past 135. The stress mounted and Costner announced his divorce from his wife of sixteen years with whom he had three children. Years early, Costner intimated concerns his career might have in the future saying, "I worry about the effect of fame on my family and losing what I've got."[24]

The next relationship to crumble was that of Costner and Reynolds. They had, in many ways, built their careers in tandem. They worked together since the beginning. Their communication remained strained even upon the completion of principal photography in February 1995 after 166 days of filming. The difficulty of the shoot was not the only reason for their falling out. Creative differences added to the struggle and devolved into a power play. Reynolds, frustrated, insisted, "Costner should direct all his own movies. That way he can work with his favorite director and his favorite actor."[25] The team was tasked with somehow stitching together the result of an interminable shoot. The final cut, according to contractual obligations, could not exceed a running time beyond two hours and fifteen minutes.

Box Office Battle

Though shooting was complete, the discussions concerning story were only beginning. The picture could be cut to tell any kind of tale. The film could be a chain of action sequences, or could be designed to reach for a more cogent story focused more on the characters. Reynolds began cutting the picture, resulting in a running time of two hours and forty minutes. His edit also presented a darker picture, a strong contrast to Costner's vision. The conflict in the editing room reached a critical point when Reynolds finally abandoned the picture.

Costner was then granted the authority to cut the picture on his terms under the agreement that he relinquish his original entitlement to a portion of the resulting profits, if any. In the original edit, the first major battle was seventeen minutes long. When Costner took over, the scene was cut to eight minutes, allowing the audience to follow just the main characters through the action. The departure of the official director meant Costner took more responsibility for the picture and these kinds of cuts. As a result, he would face the unfavorable test audiences, though Costner indicated he was happy with the end result. He explains, "I've satisfied myself that it's a good movie, you might have a difference of opinion. But if I believed it wasn't good, I'd be on really weak ground right now."[26] Meanwhile, Dennis Hopper praised Reynolds's decision to leave the project and believed the director did "an intelligent thing. When a movie costs this much, the studio and the producers come in and get involved. He turned over his director's cut and said, 'I quit. Fight it out amongst yourselves. Here's the movie.' I find that right."[27]

Many were disappointed by the story, while others were confused by the incomplete digital postproduction effects. With all of the bad press, there was little hope for even one viewer to enter with an unbiased opinion. A fresh round of editing occurred in hopes of an improved audience reaction prior to the fast-approaching deadline. Acting on the audience's reaction meant not only re-edits, but also reshoots that came dangerously close to the release date, some completed as late as four weeks prior to the North American distribution. While the editing likely improved the pacing of the story, many of the details in the set and action are missed by what all too often appears to be a haphazard collection of incongruent shots. As a result, the disagreements tracing back to the script-writing stage can be seen in the final cut. The genre of the picture is stilted, and at times kitschy.

Many critics were harsh. The preceding bad press made the few that did in fact enjoy it feel hesitant, and inferior for expressing their enjoyment. One brave reviewer admitted, "*Waterworld* is a pretty damn good summer movie. There, I've said it."[28] Another writer remarked, "I might as well come out and say it: I liked *Waterworld* in 1995, and I like it now."[29] Other reviews included as much detail on production woes as they did critical analysis. Many wrote of the record-breaking ticket sales the film would have to command simply to break even. The total cost of the film has largely been reported at $200 million. The shooting came it at 166 days. All parties seem to agree that the box office take was disappointing in North America. The careful strategy to release the film during the summer blockbuster season with a PG-13 rating was enough to open at the number one position on July 25, 1995. Yet, the total domestic distribution garnered only $88.2 million. This return has earned the picture the reputation of a flop.

While the initial release figures tell a clear story, what remains far more ambiguous is the true financial outcome of the picture. Though the film will likely never escape its reputation, it's difficult to definitively say if the movie failed in the financial sense. How can a movie costing $200 million possibly be considered profitable with such small U.S. ticket sales? The answer is foreign markets. Some have reported these overseas numbers to reach as high as $176 million in ticket sales. There were also video rentals and television deals. Additional income was found via merchandising tie-ins, though this revenue was likely small given the difficulty of marketing such a reluctant screen hero. Costner, years later, gave this direct assessment of the movie, "I think if you look at things empirically and want to talk about money then *Waterworld* certainly paid for itself multiple times, it's very difficult to get anybody to write that." He reasserts this as fact, concluding, "That was a very financially successful movie."[30] This, and his statement that "people are almost ashamed to say, I get it all the time, 'hey Kevin, by the way, I liked *Waterworld*,'"[31] perhaps indicates the movie is not as dismal as so many reviewers would have you believe.

Many have asserted that the most expensive movie ever made looks no more grand than its recent big-budget predecessors. The expectations for a $200 million budget are impossible to meet, especially when so much of the money went to correcting problems. For all of its scale and magic, the expensive atoll set is only present in the first few minutes of the movie, then never seen again. While the picture features plenty of special effects, no ground-breaking techniques were used, and thus *Waterworld* never earned a reputation as a visual spectacle. Years later, some have chosen to revisit the film and analyze it as an eco-parable ahead of its time. One writer, reflecting on the movie upon its DVD rerelease remarked, "There runs through *Waterworld* a strong environmental current, one that was mostly overlooked or overshadowed in contemporary reviews but that has been noticed since. The first thing we see our hero do in the film is recycle: the Mariner has a device that transforms his urine into potable water."[32]

The film's legacy continues to be unpredictable and sometimes bizarre. Morris Architects, a worldwide firm, has taken a cue from the film's aesthetic in a recent design. The company has identified nearly 4,000 oil rigs scattered throughout the Gulf of Mexico that can be converted into luxury spa resorts. This novel approach to capitalizing on tourism also serves to preserve the environment given the negative impact resulting from the destruction of abandoned oil rigs. Another firm, Atkins Architectural Group, received recognition in an international competition for its design and engineering plans for a resort in Songjiang, China, appropriately called Water World. The massive layout places 400 bedrooms in a massive quarry. The design boldly features the aesthetic of nature, including underwater facilities and aquatic themes.

The look and feel of the picture lives on not only in these daring architectural feats, but also in the live action stunt show at Universal Studios in Hollywood, Japan, and Singapore. The first opening occurred in 1995 and continues to run today, drawing substantial crowds, and remains one of the most popular theme park shows ever produced. It seems there is still money to be made from *Waterworld* in everything from rereleased DVDs to an auction for Dennis Hopper's *Waterworld*-themed pinball machine, fetching $1,375 in 2011.

While the production has likely now found the terra firma of financial success, one must wonder what development, if any, will occur in the relationship between what has been termed "the two Kevins." They have spent the subsequent years since *Waterworld* pursuing their own projects. Costner returned to the reliable genre of baseball films with *For Love of the Game* in 1999 and discovered critical praise with the 2005 release *The Upside of Anger*. He also pursues a music career. Reynolds has found success helming pictures with budgets in the more manageable range of $30 million–$40 million with films like *The Count of Monte Cristo*. Will they ever rekindle their friendship? The upcoming release of *Learning Italian*, with Costner as the star and Reynolds the director, indicates they already have. This time the budget is set at $35 million, placing the project and the actors on solid, firm ground.

For Reynolds, there is still magic in filmmaking. There are still stories that are worth being told. The difficulties are still worth enduring to put the picture to screen no matter how far the ultimate images have drifted from the original vision. The director remarks, "When I first started out, I'd approach projects with a vision in my head, like we'll shoot on top of a hill, amid a stand of trees, and the actors will show up on time and know their lines. It will be sunset and their hair will be blowing a particular way. Invariably, you show up and it's overcast."[33]

Conclusion

Kingdom of Shadows

RUSSIAN AUTHOR MAKSIM GORKY (1868–1936) attended a town fair one night and found himself sitting in the darkness of a theater watching an early Lumière film. The event left him so awestricken that he was compelled to pen an article detailing the experience of this dynamic art of light, expressing what he believed the new craft held for the future.

Gorky wrote, "Last night I was in the Kingdom of Shadows. If you only knew how strange it was to be there. When the lights go out in the room in which Lumiere's invention is shown, there suddenly appears on the screen a large grey picture, 'A Street in Paris'—shadows of a bad engraving. As you gaze at it, you see carriages, buildings and people in various poses, all frozen into immobility. All this is in grey, and the sky above is also grey—you anticipate nothing new in this all too familiar scene, for you have seen pictures of Paris streets more than once. But suddenly a strange flicker passes through the screen and the picture stirs to life."[1]

For Gorky, the wonder of such a fascinating invention was joyful but also dark in its conjuring of otherworldliness. His description of becoming entranced with this world of shadows seems to parallel the veil of darkness over those directors who suffered through disastrous productions. Gorky explained, "This mute, grey life finally begins to disturb and depress you. It seems as though it carries a warning, fraught with vague but sinister meaning that makes your heart grow faint."

Even in the early days of this now ubiquitous art, Gorky incisively identified the more unpleasant nature of motion pictures. While his comments touch on the literal darkness of black and white images, his figurative undertones cannot be ignored. He describes not only the "sinister" aspects but also "the energy and the curiosity of the human mind" that have made these images come to life. The darkness of the shadows is contrasted with the light of imagination.

The films chronicled in this book present only a limited spectrum of the difficulties that can occur in this strange world of filmmaking that, in its more desperate moments, seems curiously similar to Gorky's impressions so many decades ago. His impressions about film were among the earliest ever written, and since his time countless books have been devoted to exploring the power of the craft and the magic and mayhem of productions.

Though the world of cinema is less mysterious to audiences today, its enchantment is as strong as ever. While far more is understood about the process of filmmaking, the unfolding of any production always remains unknown. In the end, only the film itself is able to stand the judgment of critics and audiences.

For each director the reasons or justifications for enduring such hardship were different. For some it was obligation, for others force of will. Novelist, journalist and pop culture essayist Chuck Klosterman offered the following quote as the "best response" a director could give for allowing a film to go wildly awry: "Critics will say I lost control of this project, but that's not accurate. The reason my film became so sprawling and costly is because—for the first time in my life—I was completely in control of the creative process. The film inside my brain was literally being transferred onto the celluloid, image by image by image. It was almost akin to a scientific breakthrough. This has never happened before, to anyone. In the past, movies were merely an interpretation of what someone intellectually conceived, inevitably falling short of the ultimate intention. But this was different. This was the perfect transfer of theory to reality, and that did not come without a cost."[2]

In all of the above films the reasons for starting the picture were different from the reasons for completing it. The process of making movies continues to exact an enormous toll on the health, finances and psyche of all involved.

Notes

1. The Last Shot of the Night

[1] Joe Bonomo, *The Strongman: A True Life Pictorial Autobiography of the Hercules of the Screen* (Whitefish, MT: Kessinger Publishing LLC, 2010), 8.

[2] Roger Ebert, *Roger Ebert's Book of Film* (New York: W.W. Norton, 1997), 652.

[3] Ibid.

[4] Ibid.

[5] Frank Trippett, "Twilight Zone: The Trial," *Time*, September 15, 1986.

[6] *New York Times*, January 8, 1987, B10.

[7] Giulia D'Agnolo Vallan, ed., *John Landis* (Milwaukee, WI: M Press, 2003), 39.

[8] D'Agnolo Vallan, *John Landis*, 28.

[9] Richard Schickel, "Lightly Browned," *Time*, August 29, 1977.

[10] Alan Harmetz, "Hollywood Ambivalent as Trial Nears End," *New York Times*, April 20, 1987, A15.

[11] Roger Ebert, "The Blues Brothers," *Chicago Sun-Times*, January 1, 1980.

[12] "Landis, John: Jack Kroll," *Contemporary Literary Criticism*, Vol. 26, ed. Jean C. Stint (Gale Cengage, 1983).

[13] David Mamet, *Bambi vs. Godzilla* (New York: Vintage Books, 2007), 4.

[14] Cynthia Gorney, "Risk and Reality: Hollywood on Trial; 5 Years after the 'Twilight Zone' Deaths, Assessing the Cost of the Illusion," *Washington Post*, March 18, 1987.

[15] Ibid.

[16] Stephen Farber and Marc Green, *Outrageous Conduct: Art, Ego, and the Twilight Zone Case* (New York: Arbor House Morrow, 1988), 79.

[17] Randall Sullivan, "Death in the Twilight Zone," *Rolling Stone*, June 21, 1984, 40.

[18] Farber and Green, *Outrageous Conduct*, 132.

[19] Ron Labrecque, *Special Effects Disaster at the Twilight Zone: The Trial and the Tragedy* (New York: Charles Scribner and Sons, 1988), 44.

[20] Ibid., 33.

[21] Sullivan, "Death in the Twilight Zone," 40.

[22] Farber and Green, *Outrageous Conduct*, 151.

[23] D'Agnolo Vallan, *John Landis*, 107.

[24] Ibid.

[25] Ibid., 107–108.

[26] Lloyd Grove, "Twilight Zone Trial Ends in Acquittals," *Washington Post*, May 30, 1987, A1.

[27] Dale Pollock, "Spielberg Philosophical over E.T. Oscar Defeat," *Los Angeles Times*, April 13, 1983, K1.

[28] D'Agnolo Vallan, *John Landis*, 108.

[29] Ibid., 109.

[30] Ibid., 108–109.

2. Hollywood Be Thy Name

[1] Edward Behr, *Kiss the Hand You Cannot Bite* (New York: Villard Books, 1991), 224.

[2] Daniel McGrory , "Bucharest Pays High Price for Dictator's Folly," *Times* (London), May 31, 2000.

[3] André Bazin, *What Is Cinema?* (Berkeley: University of California Press, 1971), 140.

[4] Jason E. Squire, *The Movie Business Book* (New York: Fireside, 1992), 88.

[5] Ibid., 91.

[6] Aljean Harmetz, "Behind the Fiasco of *Heaven's Gate*," *New York Times*, November 21, 1980, C8.

[7] Squire, *The Movie Business Book*, 125.

[8] Ibid., 125.

[9] Steven Bach, *Final Cut: Art, Money, and Ego in the Making of 'Heaven's Gate,' the Film That Sank United Artists* (New York: Newmarket Press, 1999), 207.

[10] Ibid., 208.

[11] Nancy Griffin, "Last of the Big Spenders," *Independent*, July 14, 2002.

[12] Bach, *Final Cut*, 195–196.

[13] Ibid., 196.

[14] Ibid.

[15] Tino Balio, *United Artists: The Company That Changed the Film Industry* (Madison: University of Wisconsin Press, 1987), 41.

[16] Ibid., 241.

[17] Nigel Andrews, "Hollywood's Fallen Angel," *Financial Times*, January 4, 1986, 13.

[18] Harmetz, "Behind the Fiasco of Heaven's Gate."

[19] Bach, *Final Cut*, 241.

[20] Ibid.

[21] Jay Scott, "European Opportunity Knocks on Heaven's Gate," *Globe and Mail*, May 21, 1981.

[22] Ibid.

[23] David Ansen with Martin Kasindorf, " 'Heaven' Turns into Hell," *Newsweek*, December 1, 1980.

[24] Hans Koning, "Why Hollywood Breeds Self-Indulence," *New York Times*, January 18, 1981.

[25] Simon Plant, "For Heaven's Sake," *Herald Sun*, October 23, 2004.

[26] Vincent Canby, "The System That Let 'Heaven's Gate' Run Wild," *New York Times*, November 30, 1980.

[27] Roger Ebert, "Heaven's Gate," *Chicago-Sun Times*, January 1, 1981.

Notes

[28] Geoff Pevere, "Far From Heaven; Heaven's Gate a Period Disaster," *Toronto Star*, March 12, 2005.

[29] Vincent Canby, "Movie: 'Heaven's Gate,' A Western by Cimino." *New York Times*, November 19, 1980.

[30] Plant, "For Heaven's Sake."

[31] Sue Summers, "The Hell of Heaven's Gate," *Times* (London), October 20, 1985.

[32] Bach, *Final Cut*, 402.

[33] Aljean Harmetz, "Hollywood Shaken by 'Heaven's Gate,' " *New York Times*, November 22, 1980.

3. King of the Moon

[1] Buzz Bissinger, "Shattered Glass," *Vanity Fair*, September 1998.

[2] Ibid.

[3] David Kirkpatrick, "A History of Lying Recounted as Fiction," *New York Times*, May 7, 2003.

[4] Ibid.

[5] David Mamet, *Bambi vs. Godzilla* (New York: Vintage, 2007) 89.

[6] Ian Christie, ed., *Gilliam on Gilliam* (London: Faber and Faber, 1999) 3.<Au: Please provide page number.>

[7] Tasha Robinson, "Terry Gilliam," *Onion A.V. Club*, October 11, 2006, www.avclub.com.

[8] Christie, *Gilliam on Gilliam*, 11.

[9] *The Directors: Terry Gilliam*, dir. Robert J. Emery, Winstar Studio, 2001.

[10] Christie, *Gilliam on Gilliam*, 152.

[11] Ibid., 152.

[12] Ibid., 154.

[13] Andrew Yule, *Losing the Light: Terry Gilliam and the Munchausen Saga* (New York: Applause Books, 1991), 36.

[14] Film 89. BBC-TV. UK http://www.youtube.com/watch?v=kjBL5Mguv_4

[15] Steven Rea, "The Birth of Baron Was Tough on Gilliam," *Philadelphia Inquirer*, March 19, 1989.

[16] Jack Mathews, "Earth to Gilliam," *American Film*, March 1989, 34–58.

[17] Michael Cieply, "The Misadventures of 'Munchausen': How a $23.5-Million Fantasy Film Turned into an Over-Budget Nightmare," *Los Angeles Times*, January 14, 1988.

[18] *The Adventures of Baron Munchausen*, dir. Terry Gilliam (Sony Pictures, 1989).

[19] Michael Cieply, "Terry Gilliam's Latest Project Shut Down in Rome," *Los Angeles Times*, November 10, 1987.

[20] Anne Billson, "Money, Magic and Mischief; Terry Gilliam," *Times* (London), March 13, 1989.

[21] Yule, *Losing the Light*, 137.

[22] Ibid., 137.

[23] Film 89. BBC-TV. UK. http://www.youtube.com/watch?v=kjBL5Mguv_4

[24] David Morgan, "The Madness of Terry Gilliam," *Sight and Sound* 57 (August 1998): 238–242.

[25] G. Perry, "Hail Munchausen!" *Sunday Mail*, Scotland, UK May 14, 1989.

[26] Rick Groen, "IN PERSON: The Adventures of Making Baron Munchausen for Terry Gilliam, 'It was like Napoleon's retreat from Moscow," *Globe and Mail*, March 10, 1989.

[27] Robert J. Emery, *The Directors: Take Two* (New York: TV Books, L.L.C., 2000) 316.

[28] Mathews, "Earth to Gilliam," 58.

[29] Christie, *Gilliam on Gilliam*, 168.

[30] Tasha Robinson, "Interviews: Terry Gilliam." *The Onion A.V. Club* (February 2003).

[31] Billson, "Money, Magic and Mischief."

[32] Robinson, "Interviews: Terry Gilliam."

[33] *The Directors: Terry Gilliam.*

4. "The Idiodyssey"

[1] "Outdone by Reality," *Time*, November 30, 1962.

[2] Thom Patterson, " 'Apocalypse's Writer: Most Scripts Today 'Are Garbage,' "

[3] Richard Stayton, "A Barbarian Inside the Gates: Back to the Golden Rule Days with John Milius," *Written By Magazine*, October 2006.

[4] Ibid.

[5] Ibid.

[6] David D'Arcy, "Go Ahead, Pinko Liberals, Make My Day," *Guardian*, November 8, 2001, www.guardian.co.uk.

[7] Karl French, *Apocalypse Now* (London: Bloomsbury, 1998), 162.

[8] Stayton, "A Barbarian Inside the Gates."

[9] Ibid.

[10] Ibid.

[11] Raymund Paredes, "Michael Herr," University of California, Los Angeles, http://college.cengage.com/english/lauter/heath/4e/students /author_pages/contemporary/herr_mi.html.

[12] Michael Schumacher, *Francis Ford Coppola: A Filmmaker's Life* (New York: Three Rivers Press, 1999), 201.

[13] Eleanor Coppola, *Notes on the Making of* Apocalypse Now (New York: Proscenium, 2004), 60.

[14] Gene D. Phillips and Rodney Hill, eds., *Francis Ford Coppola Interviews* (Jackson: University Press of Mississippi, 2004), 48.

[15] Coppola, *Notes on the Making of* Apocalypse Now, 88.

[16] Peter Cowie, *The* Apocalypse Now *Book* (New York: Da Capo Press, 2000), 66.

[17] Ibid., 69.

[18] John Patterson, "Typhoons, Binges . . . Then a Heart Attack," *Guardian*, November 2, 2001, www.guardian.co.uk.

[19] Gene D. Phillips, *Godfather: The Intimate Francis Ford Coppola*

(Lexington: University Press of Kentucky, 2004), 154.

[20] Ibid., 152.

[21] Ibid., 155.

[22] Coppola, *Notes on the Making of* Apocalypse Now, 126.

[23] Ronald Bergan, *Francis Ford Coppola: Close Up* (New York: Thunder's Mouth Press, 1998), 59.

[24] Cowie, *The* Apocalypse Now *Book*, 74.

[25] Ibid.

[26] *Hearts of Darkness: A Filmmaker's Apocalypse*, dir. Fax Bahr (Paramount 1991).

[27] Joseph Conrad, *Heart of Darkness and Selected Short Fiction* (New York: Barnes and Noble Books, 2003), 104.

[28] Coppola, *Notes on the Making of* Apocalypse Now, 126.

[29] Robert Sellers, "The Strained Making of Apocalypse Now," *Independent*, July 24, 2009, www.independent.co.uk.

[30] Janet Maslin, "Martin Sheen Alters View on Violence," *New York Times*, January 31, 1978.

[31] Ibid.

[32] *Hearts of Darkness: A Filmmaker's Apocalypse*, dir. Fax Bahr.

[33] Ibid.

[34] Charles Higham, "Coppola's Vietnam Movie Is a Battle Royal," *New York Times*, May 15, 1977.

[35] Ibid.

[36] Leo Janos, "The Hollywood Game Grows Rich—and Desperate," *New York Times*, February 12, 1978.

[37] Phillips, *Godfather*, 157.

[38] Roger Ebert, "Apocalypse Now," *Chicago-Sun Times*, June 1, 1979.

[39] Dale Pollock, "Apocalypse Now," *Variety*, May 12, 1979.

[40] Francis Ford Coppola, "Apocalypse Now; For the Record," *New York Times*, May 27, 2001.

5. Adventure Is Over

[1] Scott Simon, "Profile: Sovereign Principality of Sealand," *Weekend Edition*, National Public Radio, August 11, 2001.

[2] Ibid.

[3] James Mottram, "Werner Herzog: 'Fear? It's Not in My Dictionary,' " *Independent*, November 23, 2007.

[4] Ibid.

[5] Tom Bissell, "The Secret Mainstream: Contemplating the Mirages of Werner Herzog," *Harper's*, December 2006.

[6] Paul Holdengraber, "A Conversation with Werner Herzog: Was the 20th Century a Mistake?" New York Public Library, Celeste Bartos Forum, www.nypl.org/live.

[7] Kaja Perina, "Werner Herzog. On Introspection," *Psychology Today*, July/August 2005, www.psychologytoday.com.

[8] Mark Kermode, interview with Werner Herzog at BFI Southbank, January 26, 2009, www.guardian.co.uk.

[9] Daniel Zalewski, "The Ecstatic Truth: Werner Herzog's Quest," *New Yorker*, April 24, 2006.

[10] Andy Battaglia, "Werner Herzog," *Onion A.V. Club*, May 24, 2007, www.avclub.com.

[11] Zalewski, "The Ecstatic Truth."

[12] Roger Ebert, "A Conversation with Werner Herzog," August 28, 2005, http://rogerebert.suntimes.com.

[13] *My Best Fiend*, dir. Werner Herzog (Werner Herzog Filmproduction, Café Productions and Zephir Film, 1999).

[14] Ibid.

[15] John O'Mahony, "The Enigma of Werner H.," *Guardian*, March 30, 2002, www.guardian.co.uk.

[16] Ibid.

[17] Ibid.

[18] "Director Interview: Werner Herzog," BBC, February 13, 2003, www.bbc.co.uk.

[19] Zalewski, "The Ecstatic Truth."

[20] Matthew Belloni, "What I've Learned: Werner Herzog," *Esquire*, June 26, 2007, www.esquire.com.

[21] Ibid.

[22] Paul Cronin, ed., *Herzog on Herzog* (London: Faber and Faber, 2002), 173.

[23] Ibid.

[24] Zalewski, "The Ecstatic Truth."

[25] *My Best Fiend*, dir. Werner Herzog.

[26] Janet Maslin, "Werner Herzog's Struggle for Mind over Matter," *New York Times*, October 12, 1982.

[27] Carol Lawson, "Herzog Jungle Film Halts as Ill Robards Leaves," *New York Times*, March 23, 1981.

[28] Cronin, *Herzog on Herzog*, 173.

[29] Alex Ross, "Auto-da-fe: Klaus Kinski's Self-immolating Screed," Slate.com, January 24, 1997.

[30] Ibid.

[31] Cronin, *Herzog on Herzog*, 173.

[32] Werner Herzog, *Conquest of the Useless* (New York: Harper Collins, 2009), 185.

[33] Cronin, *Herzog on Herzog*, 170.

[34] Ibid.

[35] Brad Prager, *The Cinema of Werner Herzog* (London: Wallflower Press, 2007), 38.

[36] *My Best Fiend*, dir. Werner Herzog.

[37] Belloni, "What I've Learned."

[38] Herzog, *Conquest of the Useless*, 4.

[39] *Burden of Dreams*, dir. Les Blank (Criterion, 2005).

[40] Holdengraber, "A Conversation with Werner Herzog."

[41] Ibid.

[42] Cronin, *Herzog on Herzog*, 281.

[43] *Burden of Dreams*, dir. Les Blank.

[44] Ibid.

[45] Gilberto Perez, "An Actor and a Director Whose Bond Was, Well, Mad." *New York Times*, November 7, 1999.

[46] Ibid.

[47] *My Best Fiend*, dir. Werner Herzog.

[48] David Perez, "Deutschland Uber Alles," *Newsweek*, October 18, 1982.

[49] Gary Arnold, "Visions of Vanity," *Washington Post*, November 9, 1982.

[50] Rita Kempley, "The Mad 'Burden' of Herzog," *Washington Post*, October 22, 1982.

[51] Maslin, "Werner Herzog's Struggle for Mind over Matter."

[52] Ibid.

[53] Nicolas Renaud, Andre Habib, and Simon Galiero, "The Trial of Werner Herzog: An Interview," January 31, 2004, www.horschamp.qc.ca.

[54] *Burden of Dreams*, dir. Les Blank.

[55] Ibid.

[56] *My Best Fiend*, dir. Werner Herzog.

[57] *Burden of Dreams*, dir. Les Blank.

6. It's Good to Be Kim

[1] Jasper Becker, *Rogue Regime: Kim Jong Il and the Looming Threat of North Korea* (New York: Oxford University Press, 2005), 43.

[2] Hugh Levinson, "Making Pizza for Kim Jong Il," BBC, August 12, 2004.

[3] Ibid.

[4] Kim Jong Il, *On the Art of the Cinema* (Honolulu: University Press of the Pacific, 2001), 50.

[5] Ibid, 113.

[6] Ibid, 113.

[7] Peter Carlson, "Sins of the Son," *Washington Post*, May 11, 2003.

[8] Han Sang-Jun, *Shin Sang-Ok: Korean Filmmaker* (New York: Pusan International Film Festival, 2002), 9.

[9] Edward Kim, "Director's Cinematic Journey Comes Full Circle," *Korean Herald*, November 13, 1998.

[10] Hong Sung-Nam, *A Flower in Hell: Fascinating Inferno of Desire*, (New York: Pusan International Film Festival, 2002), 28–30.

[11] Kwak Hyun-Ja et al., *A Woman between Tradition and Modernity* (New York: Pusan International Film Festival, 2002), 37.

[12] Peter Carlson, "Sins of the Son," *Washington Post*, May 11, 2003.

[13] Mike Thomson, "Kidnapped by North Korea," *BBC Today*, March 11, 2003.

[14] "Shin Sang-Ok," *Economist*, April 29, 2006.

[15] John Gorenfeld, "The Producer from Hell," *Guardian*, April 4, 2003.

[16] Ibid.

[17] "Shin Sang-Ok," *Economist*.

[18] Becker, *Rogue Regime*, 138.

[19] Ibid.

[20] Thomson, "Kidnapped by North Korea."

[21] Becker, *Rogue Regime*, 138.

[22] Ibid.

[23] Sang-Jun, *Shin Sang-Ok*.

[24] Kim Myun Joong, "Film Guru Shin Sang-Ok Tells of Kim Jong Il," *Seoul Times*. November, 2001.

[25] Ibid.

[26] "Shin Sang-Ok, 80; S. Korean Director Abducted by North," *Los Angeles Times*, April 14, 2006.

[27] M. E. O'Hanlon and M. M. Mochizuki, *Crisis on the Korean Peninsula*. (New York: McGraw-Hill, 2003), 26.

[28] Michael Shapiro, "A Kim Jong Il Production," *New Yorker*, April 25, 2005.

[29] Chris Suellentrop, "Kim Jong Il," *Slate*, October 25, 2002, www.slate.com.

[30] Peter Carlson, "Sins of the Son," *Washington Post*, May 11, 2003.

[31] "Shin Sang-Ok," *Economist*, April 29, 2006.

[32] Gorenfeld, "The Producer from Hell."

[33] Ibid.

[34] Thomson, "Kidnapped by North Korea."

[35] Ibid.

[36] Ibid.

[37] Ibid.

[38] Kim, "Director's Cinematic Journey Comes Full Circle."

[39] Sang-Jun, *Shin Sang-Ok*.

[40] "How Shin Sang Ok Got Kidnapped, Got a Film Deal, and Got the Hell out of North Korea," *Mental Floss*, July/August 2006, 62–63.

[41] Song A, Kim, "Publishing of Shin Sang Ok's Autobiography," *Daily NK*, August 2, 2007.

[42] Ibid.

7. Black and Blue

[1] Zoltan Istvan, "Reporter's Notebook: S. Pacific Ritual Bungee Jumping," *National Geographic Today*, November 26, 2002, http://news.nationalgeographic.com.

[2] "101 Most Shocking Moments in Entertainment," Writer: John Salcido, E! Entertainment Television, July, 2003.

[3] Philip Anderson, "James O'Barr: Author of *The Crow*," *KAOS2000 Magazine*, July 20, 2000.

[4] Mark Harris, "The Brief and Unnecessary Death of Brandon Lee," *Entertainment Weekly*, April 16, 1993.

[5] Mark Voger, *The Dark Age: Grim, Great, & Gimmicky Post-Modern Comics* (NC: TwoMorrows Publishing, January 18, 2006), 51.

6 Daniel Robert Epstein, *James O'Barr: Creator of* The Crow, Suicide-Girls.com, May 21, 2001.

7 Ibid.

8 Terrence Rafferty, "Doesn't Scare Easily," *New York Times*, January 27, 2008.

9 Ibid.

10 Bridget Baiss, *The Crow: The Story behind the Film* (London: Titan Publishing Group, 2004), 32.

11 Ibid.

12 John Little, ed., *Words of the Dragon: Interviews 1958–1973* (Boston: Tuttle Publishing, 1997), 85.

13 Ibid., 81.

14 Ibid., 204.

15 "Jesus Actor Struck by Lightning," *BBC News*, October 23, 2003, http://news.bbc.co.uk.

16 Harris, "The Brief and Unnecessary Death of Brandon Lee."

17 Philip Wuntch, "The Curse of the Crow," *Dallas Morning News*, May 14, 1994.

18 Ibid.

19 Ibid.

20 Baiss, *The Crow*, 123–124.

21 Ascher-Walsh, Rebecca, "How *The Crow* Flew," *Entertainment Weekly*, May 13, 1994

22 "The Shadow of the Crow; There Are Many Plot Twists in Brandon Lee's Final Movie—Most of Which Can't Be Seen On-Screen," *Washington Post*, May 15, 1994.

23 Baiss, *The Crow*, 221.

24 Dave Brown, "The 12 Greatest Myths about Firearms on Film Sets," http://members.autobahn.mb.ca.

25 Extra. Warner Brothers. 2005. http://www.youtube.com/watch?v=Zjn3WqsvE_Q

26 Karen Thomas, "Brandon Lee Dies in Film Set Accident," *USA Today*, April 1, 1993.

[27] Phil McCombs, "Police Call Actor's Death Suspicious," *Washington Post*, April 3, 1993, C1.

[28] Ibid.

[29] "Negligence Factor in Lee's death, DA says," *USA Today*, April 28, 1993.

[30] Baiss, *The Crow*, 230.

[31] "Same Film, Different Tone," *New York Times*, May 1, 1994, H23.

[32] Extra. Warner Brothers. 2005. http://www.youtube.com/watch?v=Zjn3WqsvE_Q

[33] "The Shadow of the Crow."

[34] "Eerie Links between the Living and Dead," *New York Times*, May 11, 1994.

[35] "Lee's Legacy: Strong 'Crow,' " *Washington Post*, May 13, 1994.

[36] "A Hero Who Cheats Death," *Newsweek*, May 16, 1994.

[37] Mark Voger, *The Dark Age: Grim, Great, & Gimmicky Post-Modern Comics.* </N>

8. Welcome to My Nightmare

[1] Ferdinand Cheval, "The Story of the Palais Idéal, Hauterive," *Raw Vision* 38 (Spring 2002), 25.

[2] Ibid.

[3] Ibid.

[4] Rebecca Keegan, *The Futurist: The Life and Films of James Cameron* (New York: Crown, 2009), 97.

[5] Mark Shapiro, *James Cameron: An Unauthorized Biography of the Filmmaker* (Los Angeles: Renaissance Books, 2000), 16.

[6] Bill Moseley, "20,000 Leagues under the Sea: An Interview with James Cameron," *Omni*, 1998.

[7] Brian J. Robb, *The Pocket Essential: James Cameron* (London: Pocket Essentials, 2002), 46. [8] Kenneth Turan, "James Cameron," *US Magazine*, August 29, 1991.

[9] Ibid., 45.

[10] Shapiro, *James Cameron*. 161.

[11] Desmond Ryan, "Tales from the Deep: Cast Members of 'The Abyss,' James Cameron's Undersea Adventure, Were Cold, Wet and Cranky, Always on Call, Often in Water, at 'Gulag Gaffney,' " *Philadelphia Inquirer*, August 13, 1989, E01.

[12] Ian Spelling, "Director under Pressure," *Starlog Magazine*, January 1990.

[13] Beverly Walker, "Teetering over 'The Abyss,' " *American Film*, June 1989, 35–39.

[14] Ibid.

[15] Christopher Heard, *Dreaming Aloud: The Life and Films of James Cameron* (Toronto: Doubleday Canada, 1997), 132.

[16] Ibid.

[17] *Under Pressure: Making 'The Abyss,'* dir. Ed W. Marsh (Lightstorm Entertainment, 1993).

[18] Kevin Brass, "Into 'The Abyss': The Excitement Ran Deep in Cameraman's Latest Film Project," *Los Angeles Times*, February 21, 1989.

[19] Ibid.

[20] "Barnes and Noble Chat," Orson Scott Card Fans' http://www.timp.net/osclistgallery/transcript990831.htm August 31, 1999.

[21] Robb, *The Pocket Essential*. 51.

[22] Vanessa Thorpe, "James Cameron: Hard Man with a Soft Centre," *Guardian*, October 25, 2009, www.guardian.co.uk.

[23] Shapiro, *James Cameron*, 163.<Au: Please provide page number.>

[24] Bob Strauss, "Actor Ed Harris Is Happy to Escape 'The Abyss,' " *Chicago Sun-Times*, April 13, 1988.

[25] *Under Pressure*, dir. Ed W. Marsh.

[26] Robb, *The Pocket Essential*, 48.

[27] Keegan, *The Futurist*, 101.

[28] Ibid.

[29] Mark Cotta Vaz and Patricia Rose Duignan, *Industrial Light and Magic: Into the Digital Realm* (New York: Del Rey, 1996), 196.

[30] Ibid.

[31] Robb, *The Pocket Essential*, 53.

[32] Shapiro, *James Cameron*, 180.

[33] Desson Howe, "The Abyss," *Washington Post*, August 11, 1989.

[34] "The Abyss," *Rolling Stone*, August 24, 1989.

[35] Ian Blair, "Underwater in 'The Abyss,'" *Starlog Magazine*, September 1989.

9. Rough Waters

[1] Sam Jones, "The Formula That Felled Wall Street," *Financial Times*, April 24, 2009.

[2] Mark Whitehouse, "Slices of Risk," *Wall Street Journal*, September 12, 2005.

[3] James Robert Parish, *Fiasco: A History of Hollywood's Iconic Flops* (Hoboken, NJ: John Wiley and Sons, 2006), 251.

[4] Jason E. Squire, *The Movie Business Book* (New York: Fireside, 1992), 27.

[5] Janine Pourroy, *The Making of Waterworld* (New York: Boulevard Books, 1995), 4.

[6] Ibid.

[7] Ibid.

[8] Jess Cagle, "Waterworld: Dangerous When Wet," *Entertainment Weekly*, March 1, 2009.

[9] Tasha Robinson, "Joss Whedon," *Onion A.V. Club*, http://www.avclub.com/articles/joss-whedon,13730/ September 5, 2001.

[10] Pourroy, *The Making of Waterworld*, 17.

[11] Richard Corliss, "What a World!" *Time*, July 31, 1995.

[12] Mal Vincent, "Kevin Goes Postal, Costner's Latest Film, 'The Postman,' Is 'Waterworld' Meets 'Dances With Wolves.'" *Virginian Pilot*, January 3, 1998.

[13] Cagle, "Waterworld."

[14] Mary Rochlin, "Jeanne Tripplehorn and the Joys of Polygamy," *More*, March 2009.

[15] David Zax, "Return to Waterworld," *Slate*, February 3, 2009.

[16] Laurie C. Merrill, "Sinking 'Waterworld' Director Bails Out of Costner Sea Epic," *New York Daily News*, May 3, 1995.

[17] Parish, *Fiasco*, 254.

[18] Richard Seven, "Kevin Reynolds Becomes a Northwest Transplant to Make a Life—and a Movie—of His Own," *Seattle Times*, February 10, 2002.

[19] Ibid.

[20] Simon Brew, "Kevin Reynolds: The Den of Geek Interview," http://www.denofgeek.com/movies/91693/kevin_reynolds_the_den_of_geek_interview.html.

[21] Ibid.

[22] Charlie Rose, "An Interview with Dennis Hopper," Charlie Rose, December 21, 1994.

[23] Cagle, "Waterworld."

[24] Pam Lambert, "Trouble in Paradise," *People*, November 7, 1994.

[25] Parish, *Fiasco*, 255.

[26] Mick LaSalle, "Dripping with Speculation," *San Francisco Chronicle*, July 28, 1995.

[27] Ibid.

[28] David Ansen, " 'Waterworld': It Floats," *Newsweek*, July 31, 1995.

[29] David Zax, "Return to Waterworld," *Slate*, February 3, 2009.

[30] Dave Davies, "Kevin Costner, Dancing with Death Again," *Fresh Air*, NPR, November 2, 2007.

[31] Ibid.

[32] Zax, "Return to Waterworld."

[33] Seven, "Kevin Reynolds Becomes a Northwest Transplant to Make a Life—and a Movie—of His Own."

Notes

Conclusion

[1] Roger Ebert, *Roger Ebert's Book of Film (New York: W. W. Norton & Company, 1996)*, 342.

[2] Chuck Klosterman, *Eating the Dinosaur* (New York: Scribner, 2009), 119.

Acknowledgments

I WISH TO THANK MY PARENTS for their continued support and encouragement. I'm also grateful for the assistance of Aaron Schlechter who made this entire project possible as well as Peter Mayer.

Particular thanks are due to Holly who assisted in editing the book and conducting research. I'm also appreciative of the editing provided by Jeremy as well as those at The Overlook Press.

Index

Gilliam, Terry, 189
Gilliam, Terry, and ad in *Variety*, 73;
  as drama coach, 82; early years,
  71–72; on film, 90; on finding
  locations, 76; laugh, 80; lost
  advance, 74; smashing car window,
  85, vision of, 91, 92. See also
  *The Adventures of Baron von
  Munchausen*
Glacier National Park, 49, 55
Glass, Stephen, 69–70
Globe and Mail, 59
Godzilla, 150, 163, 169
Golden Harvest Studios, 182
Goldman, William, 48, 49
Gordian Knot, 113
Gordon, Lawrence, 223, 224
Gorenfeld, John, 165
Gorky, Maksim, 243–44
Gorney, Cynthia, 29, 30
Green, Al, 34
Griffin, Nancy, 52, 53
Griffith, D.W., 55

Harbor Star Sound Stage, 213
Harmetz, Aljean, 50
Harris, Ed, 206, 208, 209, 214
Harrison, George, 73
Hasford, Gustav, 102
Heart of Darkness, 99, 101, 117
Heaven's Gate, 46, 47; beginning of
  shooting, 55; budget 51–52; budget
  and ego extravagances, 46; budget
  after six days of shooting, 57;
  Canadian premiere, 64; Cimino's
  presentation credit, 52; end of
  principal photography, 63; enormous outlays at beginning, 58; feet
  of film, 62; location challenges,
  49–50; payroll, 59; production
  timeline, 49; roller skating, 56;
  script of, 47; script concerns, 48;
  script rewrites, 49; sets, 56, 58;
  shooting logistics, 57
Herr, Michael, 101–02, 113, 116
Herzog, Werner, character of, 123–26;
  eye color, 143; on film, 128–29; on
  Kinski, 127, 140, 143; and Lotte
  Eisner, 138–39; on rumors and
  truth, 128

Hong Sung-nam, 157
Hopper, Dennis, 225, 230, 237, 239,
  242
Howard, Ron, 223
Howe, Desson, 214
Hudson, Ernie, 189
Hughes, Howard, 183
Huppert, Isabelle, 53
Hurd, Gale Ann, 201, 202, 204, 206, 209
Hutton, Eliza, 185

Idle, Eric, 78, 86
Imaginarium of Dr. Parnassus, The,
  189
Independent, 52
Indian Dunes Park, 20
Industrial Light & Magic, 213, 214

J.P. Morgan, 219
Jabberwocky, 75
Jagger, Mick, 130
Jaws, 100
Jeanneau, 227
Jellyfish, 230, 237
Johnson County War, The. See
  Heaven's Gate
Jones, Terry, 72
Jones, Tommy Lee, 103
Journal of Fixed Income, 220
Jumper, 183

Karlovy Vary International Film
  Festival, 162
Kay, Doug, 213
Keaton, Diane, 53
Keitel, Harvey, 103, 104
Kelly's Heroes, 23
Kenji Fujimoto, 151
Kenpachiro Stasuma, 163
Kentucky Fried Movie, 24
Kerkorian, Kirk, 65
"key man" clause, 74
Kim Il Sung, 152
Kim Jong Il, character, 148–49; early
  years, 150–51; entourage and
  luxuries around, 151–52; idea
  for movie, 150; interest in film,
  153–55; and North Korean
  filmmaking after Shin, 169; and
  storyboard conferences, 161

Index

Index